Hasmonean Primary School

This book has been donated by

Gila Gordon
Dina Cohen

PAAMON

PRESS

Clouds

PAAMON

PRESS

# of Glory

*The heartwarming, touching and humorous
adventures of two Bais Yaakov girls who
spanned the bridge between New York and Kiev*

by Goldy Rosenberg
Edited by Miriam Greenwald

FIRST EDITION
First Impression ... April 1999

Published by
PAAMON PRESS

Distributed by
MESORAH PUBLICATIONS, LTD.
4401 Second Avenue / Brooklyn, N.Y 1123

Distributed in Europe by
J. LEHMANN HEBREW BOOKSELLERS
20 Cambridge Terrace
Gateshead, Tyne and Wear
England NE8 1RP

Distributed in Israel by
SIFRIATI / A. GITLER
10 Hashomer Street
Bnei Brak 51361

Distributed in Australia and New Zealand by
GOLDS BOOK & GIFT SHOP
36 William Street
Balaclava 3183, Vic., Australia

Distributed in South Africa by
KOLLEL BOOKSHOP
Shop 8A Norwood Hypermarket
Norwood 2196, Johannesburg, South Africa

CLOUDS OF GLORY
© *Copyright 1999, by* PAAMON PRESS

Typography by CompuScribe at ArtScroll Studios, Ltd.

Printed in the United States of America by Noble Book Press Corp.
Bound by Sefercraft, Quality Bookbinders, Ltd., Brooklyn N.Y. 11232

∞ Table of Contents

Part 1

Part 2:

Clouds of Glory

Part One

Chapter One

∞ The Adventure Begins

"**W**hew! Pack and shop and shop and pack
And don't look at my room 'til I get back!"

Bleemie reread the lines in her diary and contemplated the grey clouds drifting past her window. It seemed so unreal that she could actually be on this Aeroflot flight to the former USSR.

She smiled, remembering her recent faux pas. Earphones on, she had been concentrating on a Russian-language tape. Whoever had told her that she would learn Russian this way had been sadly mistaken.

The stewardess, holding a tray of food, had leaned towards her. "Kleiner?"

With the strange harsh consonants ringing in her ears, Bleemie had misunderstood the question, and in a voice that she immediately realized was much too loud answered, "Yes, kosher meals."

From two seats ahead, a man had turned and sneered at her. Was he looking for her horns? Bleemie looked away, realizing how sheltered her life had been up to this point.

"Remember that you're leaving Flatbush," she had chided herself. As mild as this first brush with any kind of anti-Semitism had been, it was unsettling, and she hoped that nothing worse would come her way.

The events of the last two weeks had been like a drama from some novel. Two weeks ago, no one would have pictured shy little Bleemie going to Russia. She had attended an outreach convention, never dreaming that what she heard there would affect her life so profoundly. The guest speaker, Rabbi Yaakov Dov Bleich, had explained his work in Russia and outlined the progress made. As Chief Rabbi of Ukraine, he was able to describe the new day school in Kiev and the hundreds of Jewish children who wanted to learn, were enrolled, but had no teachers to guide them.

"We need teachers," he had thundered from the podium. "We have over 500 children waiting to be taught; but no teachers."

Bleemie had sat as if rooted to her chair, amazed, listening, feeling. There was so much still to be accomplished for her Russian sisters that the inadequacy of the little being done pierced her. After the speech, she made her way across the room.

"Rabbi Bleich," she said softly, trying to catch his attention through the crowd surrounding him. Embarrassed at the heads turning towards her, surprising herself, she heard her voice in the sudden stillness. "If you really need me, I'll teach."

She had expected to be put off, not fully believing the desperate need, and was shocked when Rabbi Bleich immediately answered, "Can you come next week?"

No, she hadn't been able to come the next week — it took her that long to convince her parents to let her go — and another to prepare for the trip.

The plane banked sharply now, preparing to land. Bleemie, totally ignorant of both Russian language and customs, visions of KGB men mixed up in her mind with dreams of teaching *Rashi* and *Rambam*, fantasizing about the bread-and-water diet she expected to be on, walked off the plane expecting to be in Kiev, and found herself in Moscow!

"Time for some hope and faith," thought Bleemie, who was prone to chiding herself or encouraging herself as she kept track of her behavior. "I'm sure Mommy called Rabbi Bleich who contacted someone in Moscow about my arrival. Now for encouragement. *Chazak*, onward, pioneer teacher." Bleemie smiled at her new title, squared her shoulders and walked through the cold Russian night to look for her luggage.

≈≈

Dear Family,

My bags were quite ridiculous. 48 cans of tuna, 10 pounds of cheese, 10 pounds of salami — as well as all the other things a mother would want her thin child to have in Russia — weigh an awful lot. A soft-spoken Russian woman met me and took me to a home where I stayed until a connection could be made to Kiev. Although I was upset at first, I tried to remember "Gam Zu L'Tovah," and it really was good that I got this stopover. I got lots of important information from these folks. First off, cigarettes and lipsticks make excellent bribes. I learned the best exchange rates (you get a big heaping pile of Russian money for every dollar!) Russian supper is frugal — a tin of small spratlike fish and some off-color bread, washed down with a cup of Tchai — that's tea in Russian. Impressed with my Russian yet?

Moscow makes you feel as if you got stuck in the middle of a nasty, grey storm cloud. Everything here is drab and dreary. The expressions on people's faces in the streets match the somber air, but when you get to meet them at home, out pop shy, warm personalities. Apartments are primitive, yet hidden beneath those grey exteriors, they have a courageous jauntiness with funny-colored paint. Rugs are hung from walls here instead of laid out on floors.

I spent my first day in Moscow observing classes in the seminary. The director, Mrs. Pammy Amsel, is unbelievable. I figured I wouldn't miss a pot or two in Kiev, so I donated some of the pots I brought along to a woman who just starting keeping kosher. My first donation here in Russia! Gosh, folks, can you believe it? I'm doing something really important — something vital — I feel so alive — Well, back to the mundane —

Some smart advisor had a great idea to put me on the flight between Moscow and Kiev as Galina Kleinerskaya. This saved me 70 U.S. dollars, but nearly cost me my nerves. I was taken to the airport and accompanied to the ticket office. There, with a discreet $20 slipped in my passport, my Russian ticket was approved. I was now Galina. Unfortunately, this Galina spoke no

Russian. Everybody was talking to me, and I could only stare dumbly in response. Worst moment — realization that I didn't know how to read my ticket and therefore didn't know my seat assignment. I just sat down in any old seat and davened real hard that it was no one else's. Two big hulking UGHY guys, really UGHY, smelly ones, sat down on either side of me. They reeked of vodka and were not being — um, how shall we put it — exactly fair about the armrests between our seats. I scrunched myself up in the scruffy airline blanket, closed my eyes and made believe I was sleeping to avoid conversations, but my leg kept twitching from nervousness throughout the whole plane ride, giving my act away.

Kiev!!!

At last I am here, city of my intended "do-gooding." I arrived in my apartment at 9 p.m. Do you know what my escorts went through dragging my 70-kilo suitcase and equally heavy duffel bag up five flights of stairs? Baruch Hashem, they had been waiting for me at the airport, and Hallelukah, they knew Yiddish. (As an aside, the airport defies description. I'll just send you a picture.)

I tried calling you. However, I must order a phone call — and the next one they have available is in two weeks. Therefore, I am jotting down this letter and sending it with someone who is going to America tomorrow.

Ah, tomorrow. Tomorrow I begin my teaching. All my hours of preparation will finally be put to use. It's kind of lonely being the only American volunteer here. I have to get my friend Malky to join me. Well, folks, so much from Russia.

Love,
Bleemie

Chapter Two

∾ "Ananei HaKavod"
–Clouds of Glory

The events of her young life had been so tumultuous that Tanya thought she was immune to change, frozen in perpetual readiness for any catastrophe. The toppling of all the ideals she had been told constituted Utopia, the attempted coup, the explosion at Chernobyl, the loss of her father, and her mother's remarriage had turned her into an icicle. Her facial expression was always blank, never revealing the feelings she tried so hard to deny.

Over the years there had been many changes she'd feared as well as some she'd welcomed. Today's change, however, was too great for her to comprehend — her grandmother had actually enrolled her in the new Jewish school in Kiev! Tanya turned the idea over in her mind.

Only three years ago her mother had told her she was Jewish. Jewish. She still did not know what it meant — other than that she was somehow different and that life would be harder for her. It was frightening to know that she was part of a people she had scorned. By going to this school she would not be Jewish only to those who saw her passport. Her grandmother was sentencing her to a public acknowledgment, forcing her to come to grips with her identity.

The first day of school arrived too quickly. As Tanya walked up the grey cement steps, she carefully took stock. There was nothing here to differentiate this building from any other. She opened the heavy door slowly. Inside, it still looked like a typical Russian kindergarten building, for that was what it had been before the Jewish school took it over.

By the end of the first week, Tanya was convinced that being Jewish constituted no major difference in her life. Since there were no teachers for Judaic studies, her program, except for Hebrew as the choice of foreign language, was the same as that in her old school. Although it had seemed strange to read from left to right, the new letters were no more strange to her than the many computer symbols she had had to memorize the year before, and she quickly mastered reading in Hebrew.

In fact, the only distinction this school had was that all her schoolmates were Jewish. Some had obviously Jewish faces; others looked as Aryan as she did. Yet none seemed to act differently or have any mannerisms out of the ordinary. Being Jewish, to Tanya's great relief, was really no big deal.

Russia was coming of age. It was the equivalent of the American flapper era of the '20s — a time for nightclubs, movies, and boyfriends. Although from the age of 6 so much sorrow had surrounded her that she had forgotten how to laugh, Tanya wanted to have a good time. She was determined to be a part of this wild, Western tomorrow. The new wind blowing through her land seemed to promise a future in which it would be safe to smile.

Sharing this dream of fun times were the rest of her classmates. Who cared about being Jewish? There was going to be a new Americanized Russia, and these girls would learn how to "walk the walk" and "talk the talk." It was, therefore, with great anticipation that they looked forward to the arrival of the new "Americanske" teacher that Rabbi Bleich had promised them. Jewish school was not so bad. Here they would even have the opportunity of getting to know an American.

Tanya sat in the back of the classroom, her brown eyes magnified by her thick glasses. Her blond hair was pulled neatly away from her round face and tied with a beautiful bow she had received from her aunt in America.

The teacher arrived. Grey-suede suit, high-heeled shoes, all made-up and pretty. Exactly as they had imagined an American to look — like a character out of the movies. Jewish school actually was okay.

The new teacher introduced herself. "Hello, my name is Bleemie."

⤙⤚

Bleemie was excited as she walked into her classroom that first day. She had hit the trenches, as she thought of these classrooms, and was now going to be in the front line of the outreach battle. She didn't expect it to be easy, even though one of the girls in the class who understood English would translate for her. If only she would learn how to slow down her rapid-fire delivery of lines, she would do okay. Or so she thought.

She let her eyes wander about the room, noting the heavy drapes covering the windows. She looked at her students, seated in neat rows, two girls sharing each desk. It was time to teach!

"What is this week's *Parshah*?" she asked, pausing for her translator to relay the question to the class.

The translator looked puzzled, "Excuse me, but what '*Parshah*' means?"

What?!?! Oh, no!! Try not to show that you're shocked. "You've never heard the word *Parshah*?" Bleemie asked. The translator shook her head from side to side. Then she turned to the class to ask if anyone knew what it meant. Bleemie looked around desperately. Somebody must know. But all she saw was a room full of inquisitive stares. Well, time to explain. "The Torah is divided into parts."

"Torah *eta* Bible?" ("The Torah is the Bible?") asked the girl with the thick glasses.

Gulp. Help. What now? Bleemie closed her notebook on all her hours of careful preparation. Time to pinch-hit.

"Why are you Jewish?" she challenged the class.

The translator looked at Bleemie as if she had suddenly changed into a Martian, but dutifully translated. Now Bleemie had 30 eyes scrutinizing her, staring at this strange American asking even stranger questions. Bleemie folded her arms deliberately, making it clear she was waiting for an answer.

One student decided to humor her. "Because, because, oh, um, just because my mother is Jewish."

Aha," said Bleemie, "and why is your mother Jewish?"

The class was now really convinced she was crazy. "Because HER mother was Jewish," they chorused.

"Okay, good — keep going back. Where did it begin? When did this Jewishness start?" The class fell silent. They realized they had finally been given a teacher. There was rapt, undivided attention as Bleemie began the story of their history. She introduced them to their forefathers, told them who they were, and explained the value of their existence.

After class, the girls swarmed around the teacher. They peppered her with questions, fingered her lovely suit and just smiled and hoped she would notice them. At the fringe of the crowd stood Tanya and her two closest friends, heavy-set, dimply, hard-working Toma and giggly Regina, with her brown hair reaching midthigh. Shyly they listened to the happy prattle that filled the room. The teacher had amazed them. She was to amaze them even more.

"Tomorrow is Friday, girls," she said. "Who wants to come to my apartment to spend Shabbos with me?"

The chatter stopped. The girls looked at each other in amazement. Go to the teacher's apartment! What an unheard-of invitation! Surprising her classmates, and herself even more, quiet Tanya was the first to speak. "We'll go," she announced firmly, her hand sweeping to indicate she meant she and her two friends would be coming. Bleemie, subtly aware that she had been holding her breath, let it out, and dazzled the girls with her relieved smile.

On Friday afternoon Tanya, Regina, and Toma took the metro (subway) to the teacher's apartment. There was something nerve wracking about having agreed to this deal. Bleemie had explained the concept of Shabbos to them, but it would still be a new experience.

"Since this was your idea, I hope we don't have a horrible time,"

Regina giggled, poking Tanya in her side. "You don't want us blaming you for a dud weekend."

"Okay. So I was silly," responded Tanya. "But you didn't have better plans for this weekend. What's one weekend in your life?"

"What's one weekend, she asks? Do you realize we are going to a TEACHER's apartment for this 'one weekend'?"

"Stop making such a big deal about it. Let's just get there already."

The address Bleemie had given them was in the Podol neighborhood, the old Jewish quarter where Jews had been required to live until 70 years ago — an area Tanya had never visited.

"We'll soon be passing the *synagoga*," pointed out Regina. They walked along, passing former Jewish homes that were old and decrepit, like the few old men who were shuffling towards the *shul*. The ancient *shul* itself, however, was standing tall and proud, maintaining its dignity despite the tragedies it had survived over the years.

Exterior of Kiev Synagogue, Ukraine

Tanya stopped in front of it, staring with unabashed curiosity. "*Classna*!" ("Wow! Impressive!")

"You never saw the *synagoga*?" asked Regina incredously.

"Why would I have seen it?"

"Your family doesn't eat matzah?! Every Pesach my family gets our matzos here." Regina pointed past the black gate that stood guarding the *shul*. "I stood in line for two days."

"Matzah? What is that?"

Tanya could feel Regina staring at her and she felt her face getting red. She felt like screaming out, "How do you expect me to know, when I didn't know I was Jewish for most of my life?" Fortunately, Toma stepped in to rescue her.

"Didn't you know Tanya's mother was a Communist official?" she asked Regina. It was explanation enough, and the three continued on their way in uncomfortable silence.

By the time they had arrived at Bleemie's apartment, they were far more than just merely nervous. Whoever heard of staying over at a teacher's house? They walked up the five flights of stairs quietly, almost tiptoeing. Soon they were standing in front of the door, looking at each other in trepidation. It was Tanya who finally had the courage to knock. One tap was all it took for the door to swing open. "You would think she had been waiting right here at the door for us," whispered Regina to Tanya as they filed in past their teacher.

Actually Bleemie *had* been waiting for them. She had finished the Shabbos cooking an hour ago. The army cots provided by the school were all set up in every free area of space. Rabbi Bleich's apartment and another *shaliach*'s home had been similarly transformed into an impromptu youth hostel. There were goodies on the table for her guests. The only glitch was that there were no Shabbos candles to be found in Kiev. Somewhere in the depths of the *shul's* storage room, Bleemie had dug up some old thin multicolored Chanukah candles. A candle was a candle was a candle — no? Everything she could think of was in place. Bleemie had paced the rooms nervously, peeking out every now and then to see if her promised guests would really show up.

The girls started trickling in by twos and threes. Each group seemed surprised that other classmates had come too. The next hour was spent assigning girls to various apartments and instructing them to meet at the Bleichs for candle-lighting.

Showered and dressed in her Shabbos finery, Bleemie walked the block to the Bleichs' apartment. As she passed through the darkening streets of Kiev, she felt the peace of Shabbos descending over the city. She hoped her students could feel the *Kedushah*, yet doubted they could.

Inside the Bleichs' apartment, each girl was given one candle. Bleemie then handed out copies of the *brachah*, transliterated into Russian, for the girls to use. She wondered if she should perhaps give them some awe-inspiring lesson about the Shabbos candles before candle-lighting, but decided against it.

Thirty-five girls lit a little flame; 35 girls covered their eyes; 35 girls looked up to see a sea of little flames flickering and dancing, lighting up the room and the night. Bleemie smiled. She was glad she had kept quiet. From the glowing faces, from the tears running down the girls' cheeks, she knew that the beauty of Shabbos had touched them for the first time in their lives, more profoundly than she could have ever done with mere words. She allowed them to savor the moment, then gently shepherded them out the door, to the *shul*.

➢➣

Tanya looked at "her" candle one last time as she walked out the door. She wished Bleemie would let her sit by it and watch it burn. She felt overwhelmed, not understanding the tight feeling in her chest. Even giggly Regina for once was serious, a rapt expression on her face. No one spoke, fearful of shattering the beauty.

The *shul* was up ahead. Tanya was finally going to go inside. In through the black wooden door, up chipped ugly steps, then through another door. Tanya gasped. Spread out before her was a blue-and-gold dream world. She was on a square balcony that overlooked the men's section of the *shul*. From this vantage point, one could see the men swaying, could see the carved *Aron Kodesh* with its velvet curtain, could hear the crystal-clear *tefillos* wafting up.

"Look," Bleemie was saying, pointing to a paragraph in an old dusty book. All the girls crowded around to see what was written. On the yellowed page were the words of a prayer for Tsar Nikolai. Tanya shivered.

"You see, girls," Bleemie said, the *siddur* held aloft in her hand, "thousands of years ago, hundreds of years ago, people were *davening*

Interior orf Kiev Synagogue, Ukraine
Built in the 1800s, it is one of the only two remaining synagogues. The other one is
currently used as a theater. The synagogue in the picture has become the focal point of
the reawakening of the Jewish community in Kiev and the Ukraine.

just like we *daven*. They stood here and cried and pleaded with Hashem. And now, you, their great-great-great-grandchildren, have come back here to *daven*."

The girls drifted to their own spots in the *shul*. Each one took the proffered *siddur*, feeling the weight of it, not just in their hands, but in their lives as well.

The rest of Shabbos passed by too quickly for Tanya. Three meals, *shiurim*, games, singing, and then the *Havdalah* experience, as emotional as her candle-lighting had been. She was on her way home; but didn't know how she could walk back into her old life. There was no way of explaining all her emotions to her mother, no way of making her understand that more than a Shabbos candle had been lit. How should she word it? "I have a soul, *Mamushka*, a Jewish spark." No, that sounded ridiculous. "I believe there is a G-d." No, that wouldn't do either.

The train was nearing her station. She got up and went to stand by the door of the train, watching the dark tunnel outside the window. Okay, this Jewish school had been her grandmother's idea. Let her grandmother do the explaining. Once decided on a course of action, Tanya walked confidently home. Through the door, a quick hello to her mother and then right into her grandmother's room.

"*Babushka*?"

Her grandmother looked up at her and smiled. "So how was it?"

"*Babushka*." She was crying, overcome with the mass of emotions that had enveloped her. "*Babushka*, I want to be *religosa*."

There was a silence as she thought of what to say next. *Babushka* rose from the rocker and reached for her. Tanya was enveloped in her grandmother's arms, her head buried in the older woman's shoulder.

It took a few minutes before her grandmother could control her emotions sufficiently to speak. "My father," explained her grandmother, "was the *shochet*."

Tanya wanted to ask what *shochet* meant. There were a lot of questions she needed her grandmother to answer, but for now, she just listened.

"Then my *tatte*, my father, died," her grandmother continued, "and I grew up alone with my mother. Whatever we could keep, we did. But, me, I would like to be like my *tatte*. *Oy,* a *brachah* on your teacher's *kup*."

⁐ ⁐

"Forget about the girls and what they gained. I will never, ever, forget this Shabbos!" It was *Motza'ei Shabbos* and Bleemie was washing the seemingly hundreds of dishes. Yael, one of the Israeli *shlichim*, nodded in agreement.

"You know what the strangest part was, Yael? There are questions that I never thought I would have been able to answer — yet when the girls asked them, the answers just popped out of my mouth."

Yael leaned on her broom and looked seriously at Bleemie. "Let me tell you, Bleemie, one thing I have discovered here in Russia and no place else — over here, Hashem carries the *shlichim* on *Ananei HaKavod*. You'll see." And with that promise, Yael went back to her sweeping.

Chapter Three

∞ From Kiev to Babi Yar

There were a few married *shlichim* living in Kiev, but Bleemie was the only single girl there. She had an apartment all to her lonesome self. In America it might have been considered a luxury, but here in Kiev it was slightly scary.

Bleemie went on a crusade to get her friend, Malky, to join her. Countless faxes flew through the transcontinental wires until Malky agreed to come. Bleemie rejoiced at the prospect of having her best friend not only teach beside her, but sleep beside her. As she waited for Malky to arrive, Bleemie started putting away her arsenal — the knives, hangers, and hammers she had kept at her bedside until now.

Heavy breathing. Step. Heavy breathing. Step. Wheeze. Big sigh, then step, step, step. Based on her own experiences, Bleemie was able to guess what the sounds from the stairwell meant. It meant Malky was finally here, with some very heavy suitcases that the *shul's* worker had the honor of hoisting up five flights of stairs. Bleemie flew to open the door. Igor stumbled into the apartment, dropped a suitcase, and sat down heavily on it, gasping as if asthmatic.

"You know, you should give up smoking, Igor," said Bleemie.

Igor gave her a baleful look and continued breathing heavily. Just then Malky made her appearance and he pointed at her accusingly, "Cigarettes! Ha! You *Americanskes* should stop bringing rocks here." He gathered his strength and staggered back out the door. Malky smiled sheepishly as Bleemie hugged her. "I didn't have the heart to tell him it's *sefarim*, not rocks. What's with this country — no elevators?"

"At least not unless you're a 'somebody' and get a *shtaty* apartment. How was your flight?"

"It was fine until I realized somewhere over the Atlantic that I didn't know Russian. I spent 10 hours of flight time worrying what I would do when I got here. Gosh, it was a blessing to meet Igor and be able to speak Yiddish."

"I know." Bleemie smiled. "I had that same wave of relief when he met me at the airport."

"Ugh." Malky reached a hand to the back of her neck, trying to massage her cramped travel-weary muscles. "Grime. Where is the shower?"

"In there," Bleemie said pointing. "This country has a great system. Toilet in one room, shower in the other, with very picturesque signs pointing out the difference. See the picture of a kid on a potty? That is what the British call the water closet. That door with the drawing of the person*chik* showering obviously houses the shower."

"Got it," giggled Malky.

"Now for further instruction. In order to have hot water you have to light the water boiler. Come, let me show you how to do it."

Malky followed Bleemie into the narrow kitchen and looked curiously at the peculiar contraption hanging on the wall.

"Okay. Now let me warn you to stand far away when you light it because it goes POOF," explained Bleemie.

Malky obediently backed up a few steps, watching with fascination as Bleemie tore a long strip of paper and twisted it. Then Bleemie lit the tip of the twist, and stood as far back as the paper would allow. She turned a knob and

POOF!

Although she had been warned, Malky was sent scrambling with a shriek. A big wall of flame enveloped the boiler, then disappeared. Malky found her knees shaking as she made her way into the washroom. Bleemie went back to marking papers.

Over the sound of running water, a muffled voice called out incredulously, "*This is a shower?*" Bleemie smiled. Come to think of it, it *was* quite an odd shower. The spout had to be held, which meant that only one hand was free to do whatever had to be done, showerwise.

CLANG. BANG. The ominous clatter from the bathroom was followed by a distinct, "Ouch! Bleemie, *what* is this ridiculous metal thing that *was* hanging on the wall and is *now hanging over my head*?"

Bleemie stifled a giggle. No use letting her friend hear her laugh at her mishap. She was sure Malky would have plenty of occasion to get back at her for any laughter. "That's our washing machine," she called out.

There was a clash of metal as Malky freed her head and maneuvered the thing around for inspection. "A washing machine? Are you sure? It looks more like a baby's bathtub!"

Malky was still muttering about one-armed washing and metal baby bathtubs as the two prepared for sleep. She removed her contact lenses, put them into the electrical unit that would clean them overnight, and plugged the mechanism into an outlet. To her dismay, the light did not go on. Malky tried another outlet — same problem. She looked up to find Bleemie eyeing her contritely.

"Oh, I'm so sorry, Malky! Didn't I warn you that the voltage was different here?"

"OH NO! OH NO! OH NO!" Malky slammed down the contact lens case and blew at her bangs in exasperation. She took a deep breath, let it out slowly, and smiled. "Did I tell you it was a very lo-oo-oong plane ride? I think that if I just get some sleep, I'll be able to cope with this country much better tomorrow.. Okay if I take that bed?" she asked, pointing to the divan.

"Uh uh. Not that bed."

"Who uses it?

"Just a family of bedbugs."

Malky looked around the apartment, then up to heaven as if for salvation. "And I'm supposed to sleep tonight, huh?"

"Some sleep you'll get, but not for too long," Bleemie said comfortingly. "Remember, you ordered a phone call for 4 a.m."

Malky just sat down on the nearest bed and buried her head in her hands. Then she jumped up in alarm. "*Ugh*, help! I just sat on the bedbugs' bed."

"It's okay, they don't have sole rights to it. Besides it's not so infested that you can't sit on it. Here," and she indicated the bed next to hers, "this is the best bed in the apartment."

Malky did not deign to answer, but shook out each piece of bedding before gingerly getting between the sheets. For all her trepidation, she was asleep before she even finished *krias Shema*.

True to her word, Malky was more flexible in the morning. She alternately moaned and giggled at the vagaries of day-to-day living in Kiev; but adapted very well. She boiled her drinking water, drank powdered milk, and didn't even blink an eyelash when no cars could run for two days because there was no gasoline in the city.

The best part of having Malky in Kiev, Bleemie decided, was having company for exploring. She had always wanted to go sightseeing, but had been warned that a girl should not travel alone. Now, with Malky here, she could get around. And get around they did.

The day after Malky arrived was clear and bright, and the two adventurers set out for Kiev's famous artistic area. The cobblestone street wound up a steep hill that culminated in a gold-domed church. The dome was so high above them on the road that its fierce glare could be mistaken for the sun in the sky. All along the road were clusters of houses built around common courtyards, crumbling with decay and wear.

"Malky, I know you're going to think I'm some kind of kook for this — " Bleemie began as she puffed her way up.

"It's okay, I know you're a kook. You can say anything without fear of changing my opinion of you."

"Well, this must have been the Jewish quarter. I just feel — sense, somehow — that Jews lived here. Look. Do you see those porches?" Bleemie swept her hand dramatically in the direction of the crumbling houses. "Look closely. Can you imagine the *succos* on them? Do you see the courtyard? I can almost see the children playing in them, little girls with thick tights and braids, little boys with sparkling eyes and bouncing *payos*. The parents are hurrying back and forth, carrying their chulent pots —" Bleemie's voice trailed off as she became lost in her reflections.

Malky had been intrigued by Bleemie's description, but her practical nature was always at the fore. "How would we know where the Jews lived?"

Bleemie, embarrassed, shrugged her shoulders. She wondered if her friend would question her sanity, and then decided she didn't care much. "Remember how I always say I'm not psychic, just weird? This time, though, I know. Follow me for a minute."

Bleemie always managed to pull Malky into her world through her vivid way of making things come alive. After all, that was why Malky was here with her. Bleemie had painted a picture of the Russian Jews, convinced her that she, too, could accomplish great things, and she had been hooked. Now too, she followed.

Bleemie led the way into a courtyard, scanning it, searching for a sign that she was right. She had no question about the accuracy of her claim, and didn't become discouraged when she didn't find anything to back it up. If anything, her initial lack of success made her only more determined to continue her search.

Two courtyards later she found it — the proof! Hung on the cold yellow wall was an ancient, tattered directory of who had lived in the building. The two friends stood there reading off the Jewish names.

"Wow!" Malky exclaimed. "How did you know?"

"I started by saying you'll think of me as a kook —"

"And I started by telling you to go ahead — right?"

"Okay. Let me try and explain. People would say that I had *déjà vu*, a sense of being here before, because I have these feelings. But I don't think that's what it is. It's just that a place that once held *kedushah* has a feeling, an emptiness, that is quiet and moving. You can touch it. The air is different. You can feel it in Eretz Yisrael, and you can feel it here."

Another girl would have raised her eyebrows at this explanation. Malky, however, had been close with Bleemie long enough to be accustomed to her way with words and feelings. Very little that her friend said could surprise Malky, and she usually went along with her musings good-naturedly.

For their next sightseeing trip the two decided to go to Babi Yar. As they got off the bus, they looked at the long length of road they would have to walk. The air was biting, the icy wind rasping against their cheeks and knuckles. Bleemie felt the frozen pavement through her thin boots. The two looked at each other, shivered and groaned.

"I feel guilty complaining," reflected Malky, "knowing that the Jews had to march without clothes for even a longer way than this."

Bleemie nodded her head. She was glad she had read the book, Babi Yar, before coming here so that she really knew the facts. Not that the knowledge made her any warmer, but it made it seem ungrateful to complain. As the two walked down the road, Bleemie tried making those facts come alive. She tried envisioning herself as one of the thousands forced to run down this road in the icy cold, a gauntlet of SS animals laughing and beating them mercilessly from both sides.

The two girls stopped briefly at the Russian memorial, until recently the only one at Babi Yar. Both knew this was not the site of the killings. They stared at the memorial that made a mockery of their nation's tragedy by hiding the fact that it was Jews who were the victims. They continued onwards to the second, more recent memorial, a simple metal *menorah* on a ledge before a ravine. Here into this ravine, the Nazis, *yemach shemam*, had shot thousands of Kiev's Jews. The wind howled around them as each withdrew a *Tehillim* from her pocket.

"What are we supposed to say?" asked Bleemie.

"Oh no. I don't know!"

"Why didn't we check before we came?" groaned Bleemie, as she tried to hold the book and withdraw her hands into her coatsleeves at the same time.

"I'm saying *Kuf Yud Tes*," decided Malky, her fingers turning red from the intense cold as she turned the pages.

"I'm opening mine at random," said Bleemie. She closed her eyes and opened the small brown book. She stared at the chapter in front of her: *Kuf Chuf, Koach*! "*Ananei HaKavod*," Yael had said, and how right she had been. For there, looking up at her, was a chapter that dealt with "*yordei bor*," the people who went down into a pit. Every word had significance in terms of the place where she now stood. Bleemie shivered, this time in awe of the *Yad Hashem* which was ever present for her and her fellow *shlichim*.

As she said the few last lines of the chapter, the tears started coming. "*Hoshe'a es Amecha* … Save Your nation …" These tears were a reminder to Bleemie of why she was here, thousands of miles away from home, a reaffirmation of her resolve to help the remaining children and grandchildren of these slaughtered Jews understand why their ancestors had been able to sing and believe even as they stood at death's threshold.

Chapter Four

∞ Last One Down the Hill Is a Rotten Egg!

"How many girls did you have in your class today?" Bleemie asked Malky as they let themselves into their apartment after school one afternoon.

"Only four. I'm getting a complex. How bad a teacher can I be?"

"Relax! Every day I've noticed my class shrinking more and more. I finally asked the girls who are left what's going on, and they said, 'Eeel.'" Bleemie laughed. "It took a lot of faked coughing to get me to understand what this 'eeel' is."

"I hope we don't catch it — this 'eeel' seems like a major epidemic!"

"That's for sure. You're still ahead of me, though. Today only three of my students showed up," said Bleemie as her roommate ran to answer the ringing phone.

"Hello? That's so funny, Rabbi Bleich. We were just discussing it. Right. Okay. Fine. Goodbye."

Bleemie raised her eyebrow questioningly.

"That was Rabbi Bleich."

"I heard that part."

"He said due to this 'eeel' we won't have school for a week. He suggested that we have some sort of programs for the girls who are well. Not classes, but some fun thing."

Bleemie's eyes lit up with excitement. "Them's fighting words — this means *war*!" She began to laugh uncontrollably at Malky's alarmed expression.

Three days were devoted to color war. Bleemie expected the girls to learn a lot from the activity. After all, with teams named *Torah*, *Avodah,* and *Chessed*, there was a wealth of material to be used and absorbed. To her intense disappointment, however, the amount of information the girls compiled was pitiful.

Color war over, another program was needed. The students wheedled Rabbi Bleich, and finally got approval for sightseeing tours in Kiev. The students were excited about playing tour guide to Malky and Bleemie. They took them all over Kiev, not realizing it was not a day off from studies, that as they walked they were being taught, for Bleemie and Malky told them stories every step of the way. The two even brought along a small tape recorder and Jewish tapes for stops in parks and forests.

Rebbetzin Bleich and girls of Kiev Girls' School outside the Kiev Synagogue, Ukraine

"This is Ulitza Chmielnicki," the girls said one day, pointing to the monument standing in the middle of the promenade.

"He was big Ukrainian hero." Miriam Simanov, one of the intrepid few students still well enough to come to school, explained, with more than a small bit of national pride.

"Chmielnicki! You mean the evil man we call Chmielnitsky?" said Malky and Bleemie together. "*Yemach shemo!*"

Miriam didn't understand what the term meant, but from the tone of their voices she could tell it was not flattering.

"You know about him?"

"*We* do," Bleemie said forcefully. "*You* don't."

"Typical American arrogance," thought Miriam, as she glared belligerently at the two young teachers. "They even think they know more about our national heroes than we do."

"He killed thousands and thousands of Jews."

"What?" Miriam and her friends were shocked. They knew about World War II and the Nazis. No one had ever told them about Chmielnitsky's massacres.

"He led the Cossacks. Together they slaughtered all the Jews they could find."

The girls listened in horror. They looked at the street and the monument, then back at Bleemie. She could tell they were having a hard time coming to grips with the cold harsh facts they had just heard. It was not easy to see a national hero pulled down from his pedestal.

"Let's go. Okay?" Bleemie asked softly.

The girls all turned silently from the monument and slowly walked away. Their brows were furrowed as they mulled over their most recent history lesson. After a few minutes, most had somewhat regained their high spirits, and were eagerly pulling their two teachers to another, even better, location. Surely this stop would be appreciated!

Bleemie's eyes widened in horror as she found herself at the gates of a monastery. She looked over at Malky for moral support. "Girls, we can't go in there," she said gently but firmly.

"But they have things they stole from the *synagoga* during World War II," protested Tanya. "Rabbi Bleich asked for them back and they don't want to return them. There are Torahs and silver things. It is very interesting."

"I really would love to see all those things. But not in there. I would never go into a church, girls. Anyway, it is almost time to head home."

The girls' shoulders drooped as they turned away from the monastery. They had planned two major spots to see, and both had been major blunders. Bleemie felt just as badly about the whole thing, and wished she could find a way to cheer them up.

As they came to the edge of the monastery property, Bleemie saw boys sledding down a steep ice-covered mountain. From their vantage point at the top, the scene looked like an advertisement for good old-fashioned fun.

"This is our chance, Malky," whispered Bleemie. "Let's get them jollied up so they won't go home with bad feelings."

"But we have no sleds. How can we possibly —"

"Just do it!" exclaimed Bleemie, and suited action to words. She plunked herself down on the packed snow and went whizzing down the incline, holding her coat down tightly over her knees. Malky, never one to be outdone where a good time was concerned, followed.

"Wheee!" they shrieked, trying desperately not to fall over sideways as they slid down the steep hill. The boys, who until now had the run of the mountain, stared disbelievingly. They quickly made way for the two crazy Americans whizzing down. For a moment their students stood rooted, shocked. Then they gingerly made their way down, on foot, after the two teachers.

"Well, Bleemie, I think you've succeeded," Malky declared as she scrambled out of the snow bank she had landed in. "The girls have definitely forgotten the monastery!"

The two stood there giggling, brushing the snow from one another as they waited for their incredulous students to make their more cautious way down the mountain. Once reassembled, the group set off homewards.

On the way home, the girls began talking about boyfriends and discotheques. Bleemie, ever the teacher, took the bull by the horns.

"When we're old and in a nursing home, what will you tell me about your life?" she asked. She sucked in her cheeks and hunched over an imaginary cane, in apt mimicry of an old woman, "I ched so many boyfriends, ach."

The girls laughed despite the apparent lesson. Bleemie waved a hand shakily and continued, "Chust know zat I vent to ze most discotheques." She abandoned her mimicry and grew serious.

"Or, girls, do you want to be able to say, 'I made the most of my life, became the greatest person I could be, and came closest to perfection possible'?"

"But why should I always think of becoming old and dying," burst out Miriam angrily. "I'm young now. I want to live life, enjoy myself."

Bleemie smiled and looked down at her once-elegant coat. "*Mameleh*, don't you think I believe in fun?" She thought back to the expression on the boys' faces and giggled.

"Bleemie, why you laugh at me?" asked Miriam, shyly.

Bleemie laughed harder. "Don't you think it ridiculous to tell *me*," pointing to the white seat of her black coat for dramatic effect, "that you can't be religious because you want to have fun?"

Miriam looked up in shock. True, Bleemie did believe in fun. In fact, being with her was more fun than the theater, cafes, and circus rolled together. You never knew what prank she would pull off next, what exciting notion would tumble out. Did this mean that she, Miriam, could be religious and still be fun loving? She shrugged sheepishly, then looked at Bleemie's coat again. The hilarity of it struck her, and soon she was laughing as hard as her teacher. The others looked at them strangely, but the laughter was infectious. Passers-by stared at the group of girls, two of them with giant white spots on the backs of their coats, standing on the cold Russian street, clutching one another and laughing. It was not just the usual drunken empty laughter, but a free and happy sound. And the people of Kiev, grimly rushing by, looked on, envious of that freedom and happiness.

As she walked home, Miriam relived the day's events in her mind. She had taken on a Hebrew name last summer in Jewish camp because the counselors had urged her to do so. Today, she realized she didn't just have a Jewish name. She also had a Jewish soul and a Jewish future. There, in the streets of Kiev, Miriam made herself a promise to live up to her Jewishness. Little did she know that that promise would take her across a vast ocean to America, would take her from being "Miriam the Russian" to being an outstanding graduate of Bais Yaakov of Boro Park, a sought-after match for a *yeshivah bachur*. Just then, however, in the streets of Kiev, Miriam had no inkling of all this — she just knew that much more learning and experiencing lay ahead of her.

Chapter Five

◌ Bris Mila International Style

The snow was falling quietly in big wet globs, endowing every-thing it touched with a ghostly anonymity. Bleemie and Malky, bundled up against the weather, walked out of the apartment building into a muffled city. Bleemie lifted her face up and stuck out her tongue, catching the cold wetness of the heavy snowflakes.

"Look!" Malky's elbow caught Bleemie. "Look over there!"

Bleemie brought her tongue back to a more adult position and looked past Malky's finger. The street in front of the *shul* was crowded with *frum* men unpacking bags, shouting orders, and *shmuessing* with the natives. *Rabbanim* with long beards and American businessmen shivering in T-shirts that read *"Bris Mila International"* milled about. The heavy snow put the whole scene into an unreal dimension.

"It's like being in a Jewish paperweight," said Malky. "Rabbis with snow swirling about them."

Bleemie laughed. "Only a bunch of Americans would wear T-shirts in the middle of a Ukrainian winter."

As the two girls neared the *shul*, they got more and more excited. A chance to get news of home, perhaps some extra American food — there were quite a few reasons to hurry one's step to meet the *Bris Mila* International team.

"Hello, girls," said one grey-bearded *mohel*. He looked at Bleemie and did a double take. "You were the one who volunteered at the convention!"

"That's me. I remember meeting you there. It's Rabbi Fisher, right?" Rabbi Fisher nodded and asked if they would like to attend a *bris*. "May we bring a group of girls to teach them the concept?"

"Sure."

Two hours later, six curious girls stood with their teachers in a tiny apartment, talking to the visibly nervous mother of an infant scheduled for a *bris*. Her son was the only infant having a *bris* that day. Everyone else on the list was over six years old.

Of the two rooms in the apartment, one had been transformed into an operating room, with newly installed bright lights, sterile equipment and clean sheets in a neat pile. The other room, the kitchen, held a table festively covered with vodka and *mezonos*.

There was one unexpected item in the "operating" room. Placed prominently alongside the gleaming tools was a standard-issue timeout game, there to distract the boys as they took this major step in their lives. As one youth lay down and picked up the timeout game, one of the *mohalim* joked that in America the boys were not given timeouts. The boy looked at at him, surprised. "So how do you do *brissim* there?"

Everybody in the room laughed. "In America," one *mohel* explained, "everybody is able to have a *bris* when he is a baby." The boy nodded in understanding. "I want my children to have their *brissim* when they are babies," he whispered, half to himself, half to the *mohalim*. "I want to go to America."

Hearing this from the kitchen, Bleemie began crying. She and Malky had begun to joke that they had turned into water fountains in Russia. Every occasion was so touching, so emotionally profound, that the two had become adept at weeping.

☙❧

Tanya had not been able to believe the call when she got it. Bleemie wanted them to go to a *bris*! And none of them even knew the people at whose house it would be held. It sounded ludicrous. Still, it was a chance to spend more time with Bleemie and Malky.

The three musketeers, as everybody called Tanya and her two friends, had been spending more time in the Podol section of town lately than at home.

Now, in the festive kitchen with her teachers, Tanya tried to sort out her emotions. Just yesterday, some students from her former school had taunted her in the street, claiming that she was becoming religious to get things out of the American teachers. She had realized then that sticking to Judaism was not going to be an easy course.

It wasn't easy for these boys to undergo a *bris*. It's fine for a baby, she thought. The parent makes the decision. There is no tug of war of emotions for the baby. But that an older child would decide to go through with the operation, and even seem happy about it, was impressive. As she watched boy after boy come to schedule their *brissim*, she realized that Judaism sometimes requires what seems hard. And with a shock, she realized she was ready to accept all that it would require of her.

Tanya thought Bleemie looked at her oddly when she kissed the mother of the infant who had had the *bris,* yet it felt natural to do so. She felt a kinship with her, this woman who in Kiev insisted on a *bris* for her son.

⌒⌒

With their students safely home after their unusual experience, Bleemie and Malky made their way to the Bleichs' apartment to share their excitement. Rabbi Bleich was obviously relieved when they walked in. "Where were you two? I must have called your apartment 20 times."

"You're not going to believe this. We took some girls to the *brissim*," Bleemie said proudly.

"You're right," said Rabbi Bleich, his eyes twinkling. "I don't believe it. How did you find out what was going on?"

"We saw the group of *mohalim* when they arrived," said Malky. "It was so good for our students to be there. You know the *brachah* that they make at a *bris*," she continued enthusiastically, *"K'sheim shenichnas labris, kein yikaneis l'Torah...?"*

"YEEES?" Rabbi Bleich had a way of drawing out his 'yesses' that delighted all the *shlichim*.

"Today that *brachah* had a double meaning. The girls came to a *bris*, and with experiences like this, they are coming, or rather they are already well on their way, to a life of Torah."

"Girls, your reasoning never ceases to amaze me."

The doorbell chirped and Rabbi Bleich went to open the door. That door always reminded Bleemie of the circus cars that keep discharging clown after clown after clown. At any time of day or night, the doorbell would buzz, the door would swing open, and one could never tell who would be on the other side. This time it was a group of Breslover *chassidim*, on their way back from Uman.

Rabbi Bleich settled his guests in the dining room, then came back into the kitchen to confer with his wife. "Bashy, what should I give them to eat?"

Bashy Bleich sighed in good-natured exasperation. "You don't understand that this is Russia. It's not Boro Park where I can just open something, throw it in a pot and presto a supper is there."

"We have some Kosher Delight pre-packaged food."

"That's the problem. Everyone thinks this IS Kosher Delight."

Rabbi Bleich smiled, then began preparing for his guests. As Bleemie watched, she remembered the lunch she had been served that day in the *shul* kitchen and knew she had to share this thought.

"Do you know what I ate today?" she asked.

"Pickles, beets, and potato salad?" asked Bashy with a laugh.

"No, for once it was different. Although you know, that salad is quite interesting if you think of the texture of each of the ingredients. You have the mushy potato, the rubbery beet, and then the crunchy pickles. That alone is enough to keep it from being boring. Then there is the color and the taste!"

"You don't have to sell me on the notion that it's quite an odd combination. But what did they serve today that was such big news?"

"They served this delicious-looking soup with vegetables floating on top, and I started to eat it. About halfway through," Bleemie grimaced at the memory, "I found a fish head on my spoon. It was *fish* soup! *Yuk!*"

"I also learned the hard way to stay away from their soups!"

In the dining room the Breslovers had eaten their fill and sang after their supper.

Malky couldn't resist a little dig. "Now that we're on the subject, are there any other culinary delights you might want to warn us about?"

Bashy just laughed.

The shul kitchen in Kiev

Chapter Six

∞ Of Olives, Vodka, Coffee, and Tu B'Shvat — Bleemie the Common Denominator!

"At home there is no such concept as *Erev Tu B'Shvat*. But that is in fact what tomorrow will be," commented Bleemie.

"What do you mean *Erev Tu B'Shvat*?"

"Even in America one buys fruit before *Tu B'Shvat,* but having to shop for 500 portions for the school children, being invited to tomorrow night's party at the Berkowitzes, at the same time that the new teachers are arriving from America, makes me think we'll be rushed as if it were an *Erev Yom Tov*."

"Good. Because, come to think of it, *Tu B'Shvat* is a *Yom Tov*. We had to come to Kiev to really feel Jewish." Malky picked up a shoebox and tapped on it. "Rabbi Bleich gave me all the slides we'll need for the school party."

"Then maybe we should go to sleep — we won't be getting too much tomorrow night because we have that party for all the *shlichim* at the Berkowitzes."

∞∞

Erev Tu B'Shvat dawned right on schedule. Bleemie opened her eyes, said, "*Modeh Ani,*" and realized that something very important was missing in her life.

"I want olives!" she said to Malky, whose surprise was almost as great as Bleemie's own.

Malky was amused. "Sure, just go to your local *frum* grocer!"

"No, Malky, you really don't understand." Bleemie propped herself up on her elbow. "I really, really, *really* want olives. This is serious!"

"Remind me to stay far away from you when you're *im yirtzah Hashem* married and pregnant. You're being impossible. "

"I really can't help it. I *need* olives, and I know I won't get this craving out of my system until I get them. Can't you just see me staggering off the plane in America, weakly calling for olives?"

"At least this craving hasn't affected your imagination! Let's go!" To emphasize her words, Malky swung her legs over the side of the bed and reached for her *negel vasser*. She looked across the room at her friend still tucked neatly under the cover. "We can't keep Esther waiting. Remember — we're taking her to the market with Mrs. Podolsky to look for fruit."

Mrs. Podolsky was one of their favorites among the Israeli *shlichim*. She was a motherly figure, spoiling and nurturing everyone. She was just as foreign to the country as they were, however, which was why they had invited Esther, the Russian principal, to guide them on their shopping expedition.

The two girls were soon ready for their shopping trip. Bleemie's call for olives had become a constant bleat, which Malky had decided to ignore. With the arrogance of foreigners, the girls strode into the market, ready to pounce on the best fruit in sight, but they, as well as Mrs. Podolsky, had forgotten the cardinal rule of Russian shopping: Bring your own bag! Esther, being Russian, had remembered to bring two bags, not quite adequate for the amount of fruit they intended to buy.

The four soon found themselves carrying fruit across the market and dumping it on the floor of the car, then returning for more. The ride home was quite a sight. Each time the car rounded a corner, an avalanche of fruit cascaded over the back seat, causing them to duck wildly.

Safely home at last, Bleemie and Malky left the fruit sitting in their living room/bedroom and hurried to the party. We won't go into the exhausting details of how all that loose fruit got up to the fifth floor — suffice it to say that the girls never again forgot, throughout their stay in Kiev, to bring empty bags with them when they went to a store!

They arrived at the Berkowitzes apartment still a little frazzled from their shopping expedition. As they stepped through the door, however, any trace of tiredness left them. The apartment had been transformed with a festive air. Two tall red candles stood among a flower arrangement in the center of the table, surrounded by all kinds of fruits and cakes. Bleemie checked the entire table carefully, then whispered disappointedly to Malky, "Everything except olives! Would you believe it?"

"Oh hush! Who needs olives with all these other goodies?"

"I do!"

"Well, too bad. I want some of that cake."

The two loaded their plates and found a spot on the couch. Bleemie was content just to sit and listen to everyone swap stories of life in Kiev. She knew the best was soon to come. Sure enough, a half-hour into the party, there was a knock at the door.

"That will probably be Asher," said Yael Berkowitz, as she headed to the door to let in her guest. Her voice carried through to the others. "Asher and *Rena*! Asher, how ever did you convince Rena to come?"

There was a buzz of excitement in the living room. "Rena is here?"

"Can you believe Rena came?"

"How did Asher do it?"

Everyone knew Rena was a rather timid soul. While Asher was involved in every aspect of the school and *shul* in Kiev, Rena preferred to stay at home. She had only agreed to come to Kiev because it was an opportunity to earn money towards buying an apartment in Israel.

She found the whole Russian experience rather daunting, and became a stay-at-home *shaliach*, desperately striving for domestic normalcy. Let Asher leave and deal with the foreign country. In her small apartment she tried to recreate Eretz Yisrael. Visitors were always welcomed to her haven, but this was her first appearance out of her home.

"Ooh — *I* get to tell *this* story! Let me tell them, Rena," pleaded Bleemie, jumping up from the couch.

"Go ahead, make fun of me," answered Rena good-naturedly, as she entered the living room.

Everybody looked from Rena to Bleemie, who relished her role as storyteller.

"Remember that new washing machine Rena has been talking about for weeks? The one she had ordered from Poland?"

Everyone nodded, unable to grasp how a washing machine could have anything to do with Rena's unexpected, though welcome, appearance.

"Well it finally arrived yesterday. It's a portable, you know, the kind that you hook up to your sink with a black hose."

"Well, Rena, how does it work?" broke in Mrs. Podolsky.

"Wait for the rest of the story," suggested Rena.

"Well," continued Bleemie, "our own dearest Rena was rather excited about the prospect of doing laundry as women do it in civilized countries — in a washing machine!"

"So excited," remembered Rena with a rueful shrug, "that I danced around the kitchen as I sorted the load. I even did a ballet spin before turning the dial to 'on.' "

"You forgot to tell everybody that Asher was not home at the time," interjected Malky.

"He had gone to teach."

"Yup. Rena was home alone. Well, she turned that machine on and —"

"And, what? Tell us already, Bleemie, and stop making dramatic pauses!"

"And I went to my room to dust," said Rena.

"Then she heard the banging," said Bleemie.

"Banging?" asked Mrs. Podolsky. "Don't tell me they sent you a broken machine?"

"No, not that kind of banging. Banging on her door, accompanied by loud yelling. She went to the door and looked through the peephole. Through that round small hole she saw a frightening sight!"

"Gosh, Bleemie, you're not auditioning for Hollywood," said Mrs. Berkowitz. "Just tell us who was at the door."

Bleemie had no intention of rushing this story. "A red-faced fat Russian woman. Her lips were set in a mean line and her eyes looked angry."

Mrs. Berkowitz decided to circumvent Bleemie altogether and turned to Rena, "What did you do?"

"What could I do? I put my mouth to the door and called out *'Rabbiner nyet doma'* ('The rabbi is not home'). That made her even angrier, and she started hitting my door even harder. I was sure she was a member of Pamyat and was out to kill me. She was shaking her big fist at me and yelling so loud that the veins were sticking out in her neck!

"I was scared stiff. I grabbed the kitchen knife and went to hide in my closet. I covered myself with every blanket, towel, and article of clothing I could find. It muffled the sound somewhat, but I still could hear the crazy lady yelling."

"She wasn't so crazy," said Asher. "The phone rang at the school —"

"You got out of the closet to call Asher?" interrupted Mrs. Podolsky incredulously.

"No," said Rena, "I was still in the closet when the noise stopped. Then my phone rang. It was Asher, and he sounded ready to explode.

" 'Rena,' he said, 'you're flooding our downstairs neighbor's apartment! She just called the school office, hysterical. There are gallons of water pouring into her apartment and she is *not* happy.'

"I looked over at my washer and realized that I had forgotten to connect the drainpipe. All the water from my machine ran out to my kitchen floor, and rained down on my neighbor's head."

There were giggles from the crowd, with some murmurs of sympathy for both Rena and her unfortunate neighbor.

"Well, folks," concluded Asher, "if we didn't have an anti-Semitic neighbor, we sure have one now."

"So ends my dream of domestic normalcy in this country," said

Rena. "I think I'll just have to get used to being in Kiev for the year. From here on in, you can expect to see me out and about."

"Out and about! *Oy gevalt*! That's where we should be now, girls," exclaimed Mrs. Podolsky. "We promised Rabbi Bleich to meet the new teachers, and then we have 500 bags to stuff for tomorrow."

Bleemie and Malky jumped up from the couch. Of course! How could they have forgotten? It was almost midnight, and there was still so much to do. They reluctantly said good night to their friends, and, together with Mrs. Podolsky and her son Shimon, rushed to their next stop, the apartment of the new "Americanskes."

Four new volunteers for Kiev at one time was quite a windfall. The school would be totally revamped with this new cadre of teachers.

Shimon shyly stayed in the hall, outside the apartment door. The girls and Mrs. Podolsky were invited in and stepped over the open suitcases, to welcome the newcomers. Once properly introduced, Bleemie decided to try her luck one more time. "I know this sounds silly, but do any of you perhaps — maybe — by some strange chance — have olives?"

Malky shook her head in disbelief. "You don't give up, do you?" she muttered under her breath.

Brocha, a tall dark-haired girl from Los Angeles, rose from the suitcase she'd been unpacking. "It's so funny that you should ask for olives. We do have some." She smiled at the look of delighted disbelief on Bleemie's face. "You're really in luck — we got stuck in Switzerland on the way here, and the couple who put us up gave us all kinds of food to take along. It just so happens that one of things they gave us is a can of olives. You're welcome to take it."

Welcoming ceremonies over, it was time to face all those empty bags waiting to be stuffed. Triumphantly clutching her can of olives as she walked home beside Malky, Bleemie felt compelled to gloat, "See, perseverance pays off."

"Oh, you and your olives! Can we find something else to talk about for the rest of what I'm afraid is going to be a very long night?"

"It's not just mere olives, Malky. It's a special gift from Hashem. I mean, what are the chances of someone bringing olives to Russia just when I needed them?"

"Yeah, I know. *Ananei HaKavod*. Now can we just get to work? We're keeping Mrs. Podolsky and Shimon up."

Five hundred bags later, the Podolskys were ready to leave. Bleemie felt obligated to walk them down the five flights of stairs. Light bulbs were hard to obtain, and stairwells in apartment buildings rarely had any. The only way to safely make it down the stairs at night was knowing exactly how many steps were in each flight and carefully counting. By now both girls knew the exact count.

After depositing their guests at the front door, Bleemie and Malky decided to stop off at the Smoloffs on the second flight. Even though it was 2 a.m., they knew they would always find a welcoming light there. Sure enough, Rena and Asher were still up, shmoozing with some visitors. Bleemie and Malky joined them eagerly. The topic of conversation, for some odd reason, was violent crime.

A half-hour later, the subject of mass murderers and other gruesome gore was exhausted. Now Bleemie and Malky had to grope their way up three dark flights. Asher and Rena walked with them and waited until they had locked and bolted the door.

Bleemie had thought she was too tired for words, but somehow she and Malky found themselves at the kitchen table, resuming their gory discussion. In the midst of a story about some chopped-up bodies, the front doorbell rang. They actually stopped breathing for a moment, staring at one another with eyes round with horror.

"Let's ignore it," Bleemie whispered — good advice considering that they were so terrified they couldn't have moved had they wanted to. They waiting, staring at each other, their thoughts scattered like hayseed. The bell rang again. Bleemie slowly unglued herself from her seat, and reluctantly made her way to the door. The peephole revealed a strange man standing in the hall. Suddenly energized, Bleemie ran back to the table and pulled her terrified roommate to look.

"Let's call Rena," whispered Malky, who had no clue as to who their visitor could be.

"He'll hear us and know we're home," hissed Bleemie, wringing her hands in near panic.

The only thing that they could think to do was — actually, they couldn't think of *anything* to do! They just stood at the door, clutching one another and taking turns looking through the peephole. Ding-dong, ding-dong, ding-dong, ding-dong! Whoever it was didn't seem to know how to take his finger off the bell. Who was he? Should they wake up Rabbi Bleich to call the police? Were the police more dangerous than their unwelcome visitor? After an interminable few minutes of this suspense, Bleemie saw a woman join the man. The two conversed in low tones.

"Malky," Bleemie called out in happy recognition, "it's okay! It's our next-door neighbor."

Ding-dong. Bleemie drew the bolt and unlocked the door. Malky peered out from behind her. The first thing Bleemie felt was a blast of vodka-laden breath.

"Ajsdkfjasdlfjaslkdjf," the man asked, or at least that's what it sounded like to the girls.

"*Shto*?" ("What?") was one of the few words they had picked up, and it was definitely overworked.

"Ajdskaserkasdfodf," he repeated patiently.

Obviously *shto* had its limitations. Bleemie decided that a little explanation was in order. "No *kapisch Russki*," she explained.

"*Minutechka*," said the man, disappearing into his apartment. That was easy to understand. He wanted them to wait. They stood in their doorway, trying not to inhale the stench of the hallway too deeply. The man reappeared with two coffee beans in his hand. He pantomimed using a grinder.

"Ohhhh!" exclaimed the girls in unison. "You need a grinder." Malky smiled politely and spread out her empty hands. "We don't have," she told him, shaking her head from side to side to ensure he understood.

The man's face fell. Bleemie supposed that the string of dejected words that followed were explaining his disappointment, but this whole incident had already lasted far too long. Well, if she had to bribe this inebriated native to let her shut her door, she would do just that. She ran back into the kitchen, picked up a jar of instant coffee and handed it to her startled neighbor. The man stared at her, then turned and staggered back into his apartment.

The girls closed the door firmly and redid the bolts and locks, and collapsed, giggling uncontrollably, onto the nearest bed. At last, too tired for conversation, Malky puttered about getting herself and the apartment organized, while Bleemie finished her last-minute bedtime preparations.

Ding-dong! The girls just looked at one another, speechless again. Sure enough, their neighbor was back! Strange, what did he want now? Malky opened the door. He held out a jar full of some clear liquid.

"Vodka," he said, offering the jar to the puzzled friends. An illustration being worth a thousand words, he brought the bottle to his lips and took a swig. "Ahhh, vodkahhh," he enthused, and congenially held it out to them again.

"May I never be that thirsty," prayed Bleemie silently. She pasted a fake smile on her face and used up the remainder of her Russian vocabulary. "*Nyet, spasiba!*"

The man tried again. This was vodka! Free! They probably didn't understand or they wouldn't refuse. Who in Russia would turn down a swig of the national cure-all for whatever ailed you? But the girls persisted in their refusal. Shaking his head sorrowfully at the folly of Americans, the man returned to his home and Bleemie returned to rebolting her door, hoping that she'd seen the last of it for whatever remained of the night.

Before they could do more than look longingly at their nightgowns, the doorbell rang again. It was almost, but not quite, funny. Enough was enough. Unbolt and unlock the door again. Smile politely at the swaying neighbor again. This time he bears a gift of freshly made doughnuts. What now? How do you explain kosher to a drunken Russian gentile? You don't. Bleemie and Malky took the doughnuts, graciously thanked him, and retired to the kitchen to discuss this new turn of events.

Holding the offending pastries at arm's length, Malky dumped them into the garbage. Not even bothering to cover up their yawns, they waited what seemed an appropriate length of time for the doughnuts to be consumed. By this time, Bleemie felt she couldn't look at the man again. Malky bravely went to return the dish, along with a phony *spasiba* in fluctuating tones of emphasis for realism. This whole presentation was ended with a warm "*Spkonai Noitchi*" ("Sleep well"), from the man and his wife. The two girls finally lay down to a very well-deserved rest — which would have been even more restful had it not been pervaded with nightmares of murderers bearing vodka-soaked doughnuts!

Chapter Seven

∞ A View From the Boys' School

Miriam had been chosen to be translator for a week for one of the new American volunteers who would be teaching in the boys' school. Although she would be missing class time, Miriam was so ahead of her classmates that it didn't really matter. Since making her decision to take on *mitzvos,* she had spent most of her free time with Bleemie and Malky, soaking up knowledge that would have taken months of schooling to absorb.

Miriam and Brocha arrived at the boys' building, but Brocha, the volunteer from Los Angeles, the olive supplier, had not the faintest clue as to which class she would get. They had tried the office, with no luck. No one was in there. Boys were all over, running, playing, fighting; the activity swirled around them. The two stood like dummies, not knowing where, in all this action, they would fit. Suddenly, from the other side of the hall, they caught a glimpse of Rabbi Fineberg, the *menahel.*

"Rabbi Fineberg, Rabbi Fineberg!" Brocha called out as she ran after the fast-receding figure. Miriam just stood where she was and waited.

Rabbi Fineberg halted and turned. "Yes?"

"Um, which is my class?" asked Brocha.

"You were sent *here*?"

"Yes?"

The Kiev Hebrew Day School
With an enrollment of 500 and currently housed in three buildings, the school began on this boat on the Dnieper River with this first group of boys in 1991 — the first Jewish school of its kind in the post-Communist era.

Just then another *rebbi* joined Rabbi Fineberg in the hall. Rabbi Fineberg turned to him. "Rabbi Bleich sent us a teacher! Isn't that nice?"

"That *is* nice," agreed the other teacher. "We finally get one of the volunteers. Great. Where should we use her?"

"Let's see, how many grades do we have without a teacher? Where can we best utilize her? I know, grab those boys there."

Rabbi Fineberg pointed to a group of what seemed to Miriam like the wildest boys of the lot. "Teach them *Alef-Beis*. They're new to the school and can't go into a regular class because they don't know how to read. Get them to read, so we can get them into a class. You'll be fine. I have to go to my class now. It's so nice Rabbi Bleich finally sent us a teacher —" and with that Rabbi Fineberg was gone, leaving Brocha with a sinking feeling of doom.

Miriam smiled at Brocha. "So what do we do now?"

"I suppose we, and I quote, 'grab' those boys over there."

Miriam laughed. The more time she spent with these teachers, the more she came to respect all they were doing for her community. Never in a million years would she volunteer for this position!

"Before we start, I have to know some words to control them, even if you have to translate everything else," said Brocha. "How do you say, 'boys'?"

Boys' School — Kiev, Ukraine

"Malchike."

"How do you say, 'quiet'?"

"Ticha."

"And, 'sit'?"

"Sidyet."

"Here goes," said Brocha. Then, in a voice that Miriam would never have guessed she possessed, Brocha boomed out, "TICHA!" There was silence, as the boys looked up in amazement. It was a great way to start and the lesson was soon underway.

At lunch, Rabbi Fineberg bustled by, pausing just long enough to send Brocha and Miriam to the lunchroom to supervise *netilas yadayim, hamotzi,* and *benching.* Then it was back up to teach the third grade. By day's end the two were exhausted. Boys would be boys and teaching them was a job and a half, one which Miriam was glad would be over for her at the end of the week. After that, it would be sink or swim for Brocha.

Another *rebbi,* who had some time, came over to advise Brocha. He explained the system being used in the school as similar to triage in an emergency room. Assess what a kid can do, get him to do it, and go on to the next one.

While they were digesting this advice, he beckoned to one of his students to join them. "Let him sit in your class. He doesn't pick things up easily and I'm not sure what his problem is. See what happens." Miriam, listening to the conversation, made a mental note to observe the boy.

By the end of the next day, Miriam tended to concur there was something wrong with the child. He did not sit still for a second. During the last break, he stood on a desk with an umbrella in his hand. As he jumped, he flicked open the umbrella. Then he closed it and climbed back on the desk. Sadly agreeing with his *rebbi's* diagnosis, she watched as the boy did it again and again. Suddenly he noticed her watching, and said, smiling, "*Ya* parachute!" Miriam realized that his mind was sound, and shared her insight with Brocha.

"But he's hyper," Brocha protested. "How can I teach a kid who fidgets nonstop?"

"I'll hold him down. Please, Brocha, at least teach him this week while I translate for you."

Brocha did just that. Many times during the next few days, Miriam found herself doing exactly as she had promised, literally holding him down. But by week's end, a short time by any standards, the boy knew how to read. Miriam proudly sent him to his *rebbi*. She was surprised, therefore, to see him a few days later with a group of boys cutting class.

Funny how she felt such a responsibility for him to succeed. During the next break, she grabbed him by his collar and dragged him to his *rebbi*.

"Please yell at him. He was not in class."

The *rebbi* looked at her. "I told you on the first day — he's not going to catch on to what is being taught. Leave him alone." The boy was twisting and turning. Miriam was sorely tempted to release him, but did not let go of his collar. "But he knows how to read already. Would you just yell at him and get him to behave?"

The *rebbi* raised one of his bushy eyebrows. "He knows how to read? This I have to see." He pulled out a *siddur* and opened it. "Read."

The boy read.

"*Maladetz*! Bravo! Everybody! See! He can read!" The *rebbi* thumped the boy on his back and gave him a lollipop.

Miriam shrugged her shoulders and went to report back to Brocha. A scolding the boy was not going to get, but at least the *rebbi* would see to it that he'd soon be back in his regular class.

And so would she. Her week in the boys' school was up. Wishing good luck to Brocha (who by now knew all the scary words in Russian, had gotten the hang of bribing the boys to learn, and had learned how to break apart two boys locked in mortal combat), Miriam happily went back to being a student.

These boys are davening with tefillin sent from the U.S.

left: Teaching boys to make tzitsis

right: Tzitsis — Russian Style!

Chapter Eight

❧ How Can You Be so Sure? The Big Test

Bleemie had begun a special lecture series for the high school. At the end of each week, she held a "no-holds-barred" question-and-answer session where the girls could get the information they needed. One girl, who didn't seem to be moving towards a *frum* lifestyle, always sat in the front row listening carefully. She never reacted, didn't argue, just silently took everything in. Everyone knew that her dream was to be a heavy-metal rock star, so it was with great interest that Bleemie noticed her hand shoot up one Friday.

"Yes, Inna."

"From all the lectures we've had, I see we need meaning in our lives."

Bleemie kept a straight face, but her heart was singing. It was so exciting to see that, even if it wasn't apparent on the surface, some of the lessons were making an impact! She nodded encouragingly to Inna.

"But, Bleemie," Inna continued, "what makes you so sure it should be Judaism? Maybe I should become Christian — or Moslem? How are you so sure about Judaism?"

Bleemie smiled. "A fair question, Inna, but one that deserves a full session to answer. Is it okay if I'll answer next week?"

Inna nodded. The girls left the room, arguing about Inna's question. Bleemie stood still, smiling to herself. It was so gratifying when

Girls' School — Kiev, Ukraine

the topics they discussed were not confined to the classroom. She loved to see the girls really get into the learning, carrying it with them on their way home.

Well, she had her work cut out for her. Next Friday, she had better be prepared. She gathered her books and went to find Malky.

⌒⌒

What a way to start her week back in regular classes, thought Miriam. Inna had asked a heavy question. These problems did not bother Miriam any longer. She was committed to being religious to the point of having not a shred of doubt. Yet, it was fascinating how many questions the girls could ask, and for every question there was an answer. No blind faith, Judaism. One could ask all one wanted.

As she headed down the hallway, Miriam heard Bleemie's voice. She retraced her steps and walked into the library just in time to hear Bleemie plead, "C'mon Malky, let's go home. I don't want to wait all day."

Miriam smiled. Typical. Bleemie and Malky were close friends, yet so different, like her own friendship with tomboy Avigayil. Bleemie was always trying to be early. Malky was always schmoozing and dillydallying.

Malky caught sight of Miriam. "Would you tell your teacher to have a little patience?" she teased.

"Patience!" snorted Bleemie. "By the time you're ready to go home, it's almost time to come back to school."

"You know, marriage is a lot like this. Two different people thrown together, having to learn to live with each other's habits. I thought I knew you before," said Malky in a sing-song exaggerated tone. "I never knew you were a nudge."

Bleemie rolled her eyes comically. "I agree we're a mismatch. Well, if this is a marriage, Malks, we need some marriage counseling!"

"And we'd better get it! We're too different to be compatible."

"Yet isn't it funny that you two deal so well together?" Miriam asked thoughtfully.

"This is dealing well together?" asked Malky in mock horror.

"Well, you accomplish so much together."

"Only because of the *Ananei HaKavod*."

"Yes, any accomplishments made are purely from Hashem. And I'm *davening* for Divine intervention in handling today's question."

"Why? What was today's question?" asked Malky.

"Please tell her later," said Miriam. "Bleemie, I have to speak to you."

"Speak on, my dear."

"You know that boy Tolik?"

"The one who walks two miles every Shabbos to come to *shul*?"

"Yes. He started keeping kosher, Bleemie, and he has nothing to eat. He only eats potatoes, and he cooks them by holding them over the burner because he has no *kosher* pots."

"*Oy vey!* Tell him to come to the *shul* kitchen every Friday. I'll prepare a bag of food for him every week."

"Thanks, Bleemie. What about pots and dishes?"

"Don't worry, *Mameleh*. Consider it taken care of. Tolik will have everything he needs. Now, Malky, let's skeddadle home."

⌒⌒

For the next week, Malky was rebuffed every time she attempted to speak to Bleemie about anything other than Jewish history. Malky couldn't wait for the next lecture to be delivered. Talk in the apartment revolved around the fact that the missionaries, with un-limited resources, were hard at work in Kiev, while the *frum* community had barely enough funds to make ends meet.

Friday morning, Bleemie awoke early. Too tense to sleep any more, she nudged Malky awake. "Christianity, here I come," she announced.

Malky groaned. "I can't wait until this afternoon."

"Oh, don't be so optimistic. You never know what question will be asked *this* week."

"Go ahead. Scare me, Bleemie."

Despite all her grousing, Malky was even more absorbed in her students than was her friend. Since she had come to Kiev, the whole world had ceased to exist. All that mattered, and mattered deeply, was that her students should understand and learn. As much as they teased one another, and as much as their styles differed, both girls were united by their burning desire to make an impact in Kiev.

Bleemie walked into the classroom, checking to see that Inna was sitting in her usual spot, pen poised over paper. Today, every girl was attentive, curious as to how Bleemie would answer the question.

⌒⌒

Miriam was surprised as the lesson progressed. Bleemie did not, as all the girls had imagined she would, compare religions. Instead, she traced their histories from formation through adaptions and growth. An hour passed by without one interruption, just total un-divided attention. Miriam kept glancing over at Inna, trying to gauge her reaction. Inna sat, as usual, her expression unwavering. Her brown eyes never left Bleemie's face, her hand scribbled away furi-ously; but her face betrayed nothing.

After the lecture, the girls surrounded Bleemie, asking questions and discussing the impact of what she had said. Miriam sat happily at her desk. She was pretty sure that today's lecture would help more girls become committed to the Jewish way of life. Soon the *frum* girls would have strength in numbers.

⌒⌒

As the crowd around her desk thinned, Bleemie saw Inna standing there, pen and pad in hand. She walked over to her and smiled. "Well, Inna, was your question answered?"

"Um, yes. Now I understand. Bleemie, could you please tell me how I go about keeping kosher?"

As much as she was used to the determination and commitment of the Russian Jews and their unquenchable thirst for truth, this time Bleemie's jaw dropped. She was in awe of such strength of character. Inna had needed to know if Torah was true. And since it was, she had no choice but to accept it, for truth is an unyielding reality, and its seekers must mold themselves to its patterns. Inna, once sure of what was real and true, was willing to go to any lengths to live up to its demands.

Bleemie could just marvel at such greatness, feeling that she was far from that level. She was unaware of the tremendous personal growth she had accomplished in the short time she'd been in Kiev. She thought of herself as a true *Galus* Jew, too caught up in the luxuries that America offered to accept the fact that truth is not dependent on comfort or ease. It stands on its own. And one who truly seeks it treasures it.

Chapter Nine

∞ All Fluff, but Lots of Substance

"You know what I need right now?" asked Malky.

"A Porsche?"

"A *Porsche*?! Maybe a Lambergini but not a Porsche. Actually all I need right now is a little bit of Mrs. Podolsky's home-cooking."

"MSG getting you down?"

"Instant soup and instant oatmeal are okay up until a point."

It didn't take too long to conclude that it was time to visit the Podolskys. That warm and welcoming lady always had something good to eat, even for the unexpected visitor.

As Bleemie and Malky knocked at the open door of his apartment, Rabbi Podolsky waved them in, continuing a phone conversation with what seemed to be the *shochet*.

"Two ducks and, one minute — Ima, how many chickens?"

"Two chickens," said Mrs. Podolsky, emerging with dripping hands from the tiny, boxlike kitchen.

"Two chickens," said Rabbi Podolsky, "and a giraffe...Yes it's kosher, we just don't know where to *shecht* it —"

"Abba, can we get the ducks live?" asked Shimon, breaking into his father's conversation.

His mother looked at him. "What would you do with live ducks?"

"Keep them as pets."

His mother's eyes scanned her all-too-small apartment. She laughed ruefully and returned to her kitchen. Shimon sighed and looked at the two girls, as if asking for their support.

Bleemie looked at Malky and raised one eyebrow. Malky knew that look — it meant some sort of plan that she might not necessarily want to be involved in. This time she was lucky — the only thing she had to volunteer was her creativity. Putting their hunger aside, the two girls went back to their apartment, to return a few minutes laters, each with a hand held mysteriously behind her back.

"We have a present for Shimon," Malky explained.

Mrs. Podolsky looked surprised, but called to her son to join them.

"Here, Shimon," said Bleemie as she and Malky held magnetic, "popsicle" arts-and-crafts projects vaguely resembling a duck and a giraffe, "these are for you."

"Uh, thank you," said a clearly bewildered and unimpressed young man. He never had understood the female psyche, and this little incident went far towards reinforcing his conviction that he never would!

Monday was market day, and Bleemie decided to go. Too many hours of lesson planning meant staying in the stuffy apartment and getting a headache. A little fresh air always helped her resume work with more enthusiasm.

The usual sights greeted her at the bazaar, the small mounds of fruits and vegetables on counters near outdated, rickety scales left over from some bygone era. Behind them hung carcasses of dead animals. Customers would point to the particular cut of meat they wanted and the butcher would obligingly hack it off for them, startling the flies who had assumed they had first dibs on it. All around the periphery of the market were various booths and vendors selling an assortment of all kinds of goods.

"Oh no," thought Bleemie, "I forgot to bring a bag again." Bags were a rare commodity in Ukraine, next to impossible to get. Well, she wasn't really here to buy, just to air out her mind. She loved the market, loved watching the Russian Orientals, their skin looking like the dried prunes and apricots they presided over.

Her muscles relaxed, her mind free of worries, Bleemie was ready to head back home when she spotted them — a box full of cheeping, yellow fluff balls hopping about at the feet of a gnarled old Russian *babushka.* "*Skolka?*" she asked, without time for thought or reflection.

"Two for 10 rubles," said the woman, holding up her gnarled fingers to make her price clear.

Bleemie handed the woman 10 rubles, then bent down and scooped up two of the cheeping chicks. As she headed for the door of the bazaar she suddenly realized the two chicks would not appreciate the extreme cold outside. Bleemie bit her lip and stood there, holding the two wriggling things, their heartbeat soft and quick against her palm.

For lack of a better solution, she gently placed them into her coat pockets, one on each side, and walked towards the warmth of home as quickly as she could without running. Bleemie noticed passers-by looking at her strangely, and thought of meowing to confuse them even more. She decided, however, that the cheeping from her pockets was calling enough attention to herself on the staid street of Kiev — no need to go overboard! She headed straight for the Podolskys.

"*Shalom,* Bleemie," said Mrs. Podolsky, in her usual warm, motherly way.

"Is Shimon here?"

Mrs. Podolsky remembered the last time that question had been asked, and how Shimon had wondered about the sanity of her two American co-teachers. She was too polite, however, to let the girls know of his reaction.

"Shimon," she called, "there's someone here to see you."

Shimon emerged from his room, book in hand. "Who?" he asked, then caught sight of Bleemie. His expression took on a guarded polite glaze.

"I have a present for you."

Shimon smiled politely, bracing himself to look pleased at yet another babyish, ridiculous gift.

Until this point, Bleemie had kept her hands in her pockets, covering the now-sleeping chicks. As she withdrew them and set them gently down, they awoke and, free at last of her linty pocket, hopped and peeped, pecking at the floor.

Shimon was too entranced to even thank her. He was busy holding the chickens, petting them and laughing as they poked and scratched at his hands. Bleemie looked cautiously at Mrs. Podolsky, a bit fearful that the usually easygoing woman might be upset — might even tell her to take her silly chickens and leave.

Somehow, Bleemie almost hoped that she would. She half-liked the idea of a pet herself. She was startled to see Mrs. Podolsky smile indulgently.

"Shimon, now you have another *mitzvah* — feeding the chickens before you eat!"

From the Podolskys, Bleemie went back to her apartment to oversee a *Bikur Cholim* project which she had set up with her students. That completed, she called Miriam to ask her to meet her in the *shul* in the morning. Tomorrow would be an early start. A *bar mitzvah* was scheduled for 7 a.m., and Bleemie had agreed to set up a party in honor of the occasion.

By a quarter of 7 the next morning, Bleemie had the room set up festively. The guests started to trickle in and the party was presently in full swing. It was a true Kiev-ish *bar mitzvah*, complete with tuna fish, cookies, compote, and fruit. Of course, the boy's family brought along the requisite Russian vodka.

A group of boys who have just celebated their bar mitzvah with Rabbi Barkan in Riga, 1996

It was times like these that made Bleemie pity all her friends who had not taken the opportunity to teach in Kiev. There were *mitzvos* here everywhere just for the taking. In a mere two days, she could grab thousands of *mitzvos*. She could run from night classes to *bar mitzvos*, from day classes to *brissim* — this land was a virtual "*Chap-a-Mitzvah*" land.

Kiev was also a learning experience. A festive celebration like the one this morning helped her to really understand the essence of *sim-chah*. It was not a big catering hall, beautiful bouquets of flowers, not even elegant dresses. A *simchah* here in Kiev lived up to its name — pure unadulterated happiness at something profound, untarnished by *narishkeit*. Everybody at these *simchos* understood what was being celebrated, and participated in that joy.

Pity the poor American girls who sat "sheltered" in their homes, who never would blossom with the outpouring of giving they could accomplish in Russia.

Chapter Ten

∞ Under the Chuppah

All the teachers had gathered in one of the apartments to prepare their lessons. They usually spent two hours a day together right before night classes. This way, they could help each other out with ideas and get a chance to catch up on the latest goings-on.

"The girls will be here in another 45 minutes," said Bleemie, glancing at her watch. "Oh no, I've got to make them something to eat." She hurried away to the kitchen to work her culinary magic! The girls who came for night classes ate supper before classes began and so a decent meal became important.

Bleemie started rummaging in the cabinets. With dismay she realized she hadn't restocked her food supply in a long time. Her salami and cheese had long been gone, and now she was out of eggs. Her search turned up some canned vegetables, a can of tomato sauce, and tuna fish.

"Necessity is the mother of invention," she thought, as she combined the three in a pot and put it up to warm. Crackers she had in abundance, as well as punch, to round out the meal.

The best thing Bleemie could say about the concoction was that it didn't take long to cook. By the time the girls arrived, Bleemie's gourmet meal was done. Proud of her inventiveness, she carried it into the dining room where their night students sat. Her five co-teachers wrinkled their noses and raised their eyebrows at her in horror. Ignoring them, she set the steaming mess on the table. In no time at all it was gone, with compliments to the cook from the Russian girls.

"How do girls in America learn to cook?" asked one of the student guests. "You have such nice recipes!"

"We experiment on our new husbands," giggled Bleemie. "They have to put up with us until we learn. We don't experiment on them until we're safely married to them — and there's always take-out food!"

Bleemie smilingly explained the food scene in the *frum* communities in the U.S. to the amazed audience. So much kosher food available — restaurants, caterers, fast-food spots — what heaven!

The chatter about new husbands, take-out food, catering, establishments, and pizza stores suddenly turned serious — as these discussions so often did.

"But how do you get to meet your husband if you don't have boyfriends?" asked one young lady with a pensive look in her eye "Uh, oh! It's time to get down to brass tacks," thought Malkie. "No more beating around the bush. But while I do my thing, how can I make them see the beauty of our way of life, and the happiness it brings?"

As the teachers cleared up after night classes, Bleemie had a sudden realization. "You know I just realized that these girls don't even know what a Jewish wedding is all about," she announced. "They have never seen one!"

Bleemie's observation echoed round the room, and the six teachers thought about it.

"Maybe when I get engaged, I can convince my *chasan* to come here to get married," said Tzippy.

"You're expecting too much of a guy. I agree he'd have to be somewhat adventurous to marry you," teased Chanie, "but how daring can you expect him to be?"

Malky was ever the thrifty practical one. "Well, it would certainly be cheaper to get married here."

"Sure, provided you didn't want your family to be at your wedding. Can you imagine telling them you've decided to get married thousands of miles away?"

"A mock wedding!" suddenly exclaimed Tova. "That's what we need!"

Of course. And a mock wedding was exactly what Kiev was going to have. Tova was able to find what passed as a wedding gown for $20, and live flowers for another $5. She had insisted on bringing her keyboard with her to Russia, and now it would stand her in good stead. Bleemie raided everyone's pantries for cookies and candies. She borrowed the *chuppah* from the *shul's* storage room. A mock *kesubah* was written, a *kiddush* cup located, and a cheap ring bought. The hands-on lesson was about to begin.

The night before the "wedding" all the teachers piled into a car and went back into the school building. They decorated the lunch room with streamers, balloons, and flowers. The tables were decked with tablecloths highlighted by beautiful floral centerpieces. A school chair was festooned with crepe paper for the *kallah*. Although it was already late, there were waitress uniforms to be made, the gown to be lined so as to be *tzniusdik*, and a crepe-paper flower bouquet to create.

Four a.m., six happy teachers fell into bed. At the crack of dawn, they left their apartments to head back to school again. They wanted to be there to greet the girls.

Tanya had been looking forward to this day. For the past week, all talk had revolved around the mock wedding. Lena was to be the *chasan* and *Toma* the *kallah*. The three musketeers, as Bleemie called them, walked up to the school building.

Tanya blinked her eyes rapidly behind her thick glasses at the sight that met her as they walked in. Gone were the drab, ordinary walls and rooms. The school had been transformed into a gaily bedecked hall. Upstairs, in the auditorium, there stood a tall velvet canopy. Downstairs, in the lunchroom, the tables were set for a banquet, with live flowers adorning each one.

The ceremony was fittingly solemn. The young "couple" stood underneath the *chuppah*, listening to Rav Bleich explain the significance of the moment. The witnesses were called up, and the most advanced students were given the honor of reciting the *brachos*. Rabbi Bleich declared the "couple" happily married, and the whole wedding party trooped downstairs for a meal that the teachers had explained was a *mitzvah* to eat. There was so much information to register, so many new *halachos* to be learned, all from a mock wedding!

After the meal, Tova began to play lively wedding tunes. The American teachers, usually so serious in this building, insisted that everybody join in the dancing. Shyly, the girls stood on the sidelines, watching in amazement as their teachers danced, and finally allowed themselves, one by one, to be pulled into the fast-moving circle. Their Russian teachers, however, maintained their dignity, and refused to join.

"C'mon. You have to be *b'simchah*," Bleemie insisted, grabbing hold of their hands. She tugged, she pulled, she persevered and she won!

The Russian teachers joined the fast-moving whirl. Bleemie went into the center of the circle and did some fancy footwork. Faster, faster! You can be *frum* and dance better than any disco-goer. Watch me. Here's a new step. Now for the *kazatzke!*

The girls warmed to the action. Holding hands with her friends, Tanya watched her American teachers reaching through to her Russian teachers. She felt a warmth, a sense of belonging, and a smile tugged at her lips. It was the first time she had smiled in six years.

In the center of the circle, Toma held a decorated umbrella high over her head. Each of her friends was holding one of the streamers that were attached to it. The whole day had been one Toma was never going to forget.

This morning, for the first time, she had enjoyed *davening*. Until now her lessons had been data, information handed to her. Something about today had connected her mind with her heart. She felt her Jewishness keenly, and knew that when she did get married she would be having just this kind of wedding. She looked up at the umbrella.

A thought that she wanted to remember to share with Bleemie popped into her head. The umbrella was symbolic of the Torah, upheld proudly by *frum* people. The streamers were those people reaching out to her community. See, all her friends wanted to grasp the bright ribbons. They wanted to attach themselves to the Torah. She watched them clutching the bits of streamers in their hands, dancing around her. *Baruch Hu Elokeinu Shebranu Lichvodo.*

The dance was over, but Toma stood as if rooted, holding the umbrella over her head. She was stretching the moment out, wanting it to be etched onto her mind. Her heart overflowed. She looked up at the umbrella again, raised it as if to salute, then looked up beyond the umbrella.

"I want to be attached to Your Torah, to hold it up high," she whispered. Nobody noticed her *davening* there on the chair. *Tefillah*, communication to *Hashem* — she had mastered that and so many other lessons today. But enough — her friends were waiting for her to join in a line dance. She caught up the gown in one hand and jumped off the chair.

Mrs. Petrova stood safely behind a table. All of her colleagues were out on the dance floor, looking ridiculous in front of their students. Not she! She just kept clear of that crazy, wild American who had pulled the rest of the teaching staff into this display of wildness.

It was an intriguing sight, she had to admit, one rarely seen in her country, to see so many people happy, laughing and acting carefree. She didn't notice Bleemie's approach until she felt her hands being held. She stared into the girl's flushed, smiling face.

Dancing at the mock wedding

"The *kazatzka*, Mrs. Petrova," Bleemie offered.

She could not imagine why she allowed herself to be led into the middle of the circle, or what made her agree to get down on the floor to illustrate a proper *kazatzka*. She felt ridiculous. This was no place for a dignified woman like her. And yet, suddenly, Mrs. Petrova felt at peace with what she was doing. She had suffered enough during her lifetime for being Jewish. Schools, careers, desirable positions had been denied to her because she was a Jew. It was time to find the joy in her identity — time to kick up her heels and sing, like these Americans, "*Ochen Chaslivi Ya Patamushta Ya Ivri!*" ("I am happy because I am a Jew!") She tucked in the bun at the back of her head more tightly, smiled at Bleemie and began to dance in earnest.

These youngsters had given her the gift of herself.

Chapter Eleven

∞ A Taste of Shabbos

Brocha poked her head into the *shul* kitchen one Friday afternoon, then whispered over her shoulder, "Watch out, guys. I've never seen her peel this fast."

"Uh, oh. Should we wait until all her steam is used up on those potatoes or should we apologize now?" asked Tova.

"I say we wait."

"No, she'll become doubly angry. Let's go," said Malky, waving the other teachers in.

"She" was Bleemie, who ignored the other girls as they filed into the kitchen. The click, click of her peeler sounded loud in the silence. Her eyes flashed like the silver of the peeler in the sun.

Tzippy cleared her throat. "Um, what do you want us to do?"

"Do?" asked Bleemie. "Why — would — you — trouble — yourselves — doing — *anything*?" Each word was enunciated clearly and underscored with a flying potato peel. "I — can — handle — *everything*." Bleemie clamped her mouth shut, and peels flew in all directions.

"Oh, Bleemie, come on! We understand why you're angry at us," said Malky. "We're sorry we didn't help out at first, but now that we're here, tell us what to do."

"Okay," said Bleemie with a sigh and a shrug. "Check the beans for the *chulent* and peel the carrots."

The girls smiled in relief and set to work. This scene was not unusual on Friday afternoons. Bleemie was a pro in the kitchen and began working immediately after school. The other teachers would often get sidetracked and then have to deal with Bleemie's temper. Luckily for all, Bleemie was quick to forgive. The kitchen was quiet now, as they waited for her to calm down. It was not long before she gave a low chuckle.

"What's so funny?" asked Leah quickly, happy to break the uncomfortable silence.

"Look in those boxes."

Leah opened a box flap and peered inside. "Glasses — what's so funny about that?"

"When I wrote out the shopping list today, I forgot the Russian word for plastic cups. I know I'm not an artist, but I was sure I could at least draw a cup — so I drew one. I thought it strange when Edik asked me how many I needed. I didn't realize what he thought I meant, and said, '*Mnoga, mnoga*—many, many!' Sure enough, we now have many, many glasses."

"Oh, no, now we've got to *toivel* them."

"Never mind — we have a more serious problem this week than cups," said Tzippy.

"Don't remind us," said Brocha glumly. "There is nothing we can do about it."

The Shabbos program had become very popular and the number of girls attending grew larger each week. The lack of beds and bedding caused the six teachers many problems. This week they had lost count of how many girls they had invited, and did not know what would happen that night when it came time to assign beds.

Sundown came to Kiev. Bleemie was always amazed at the magic Shabbos wrought. During the day she could be short tempered, grimy, and overwhelmed. Instantly, as soon as Shabbos arrived, an inner peace would take over and she felt regal.

After the *seudah* and the singing, it was time to match their guests with their sleeping arrangements. Every bed and cot, every couch and pillow, was soon occupied. Finally, three teachers were left to crowd into one bed, which left the other three —

"Don't let them know we have nowhere to sleep," whispered Bleemie.

"So what are we going to do?" asked Brocha, laughing at their ludicrous situation.

"We'll put blankets on the floor of the kitchen and sleep there," suggested Tzippy. Each girl took her blanket and tried to walk into the kitchen as unobtrusively as possible.

"Lock the door," whispered Bleemie. "The girls will feel guilty if they see how we're sleeping."

The door was latched, and each of the three arranged her blanket on the floor. Tzippy began giggling. Trust Tzippy to always giggle.

"Okay, one, two, three, here we go," said Tzippy. On cue, all three settled down on the blankets. There was a lot of rolling and moving about as each tried to stretch out full length, only to realize the futility of the attempt. They had overlooked the size of the kitchen, a two-by-two cubicle which didn't have enough space for them to stretch out their legs.

Brocha put her feet on the wall at first, then gave up and opted to do as the others did — bending her feet at the knees. There they lay, head to head, giggling, with their legs bent, but their souls happy. More time was spent giggling that night than sleeping.

"Yom zeh mechubad mikal..." In the peace that only Shabbos wrought, the voices of 70 girls blended together in the *shul* lunchroom.

"Crash!" A rock flew through the stained-glass window and fell with a loud thud in the center of one of the tables. The girls screamed and ran to the far end of the room. Bleemie stared in disbelief at the jagged hole left by the rock. She hurried out to the roof to catch sight of the hoodlums who had done the mischief, but they were gone. All was quiet in the streets of Kiev, the ominous quiet of indifference.

Bleemie turned and went back into the lunchroom. Where a few minutes ago had been a serene Shabbos scene, there now was a tumult of girls milling about.

"Girls," Bleemie called for attention. The girls looked up at her, sadness in their young eyes.

"Girls, they wanted to disturb our Shabbos, but we won't let them win." Picking up a board, Bleemie walked determinedly over to the jagged hole. She placed the board against the window, blocking the opening, shielding her girls from any future rocks. Then she sat down in her seat and picked up the tune they had been singing. Slowly but surely, all the girls found their seats and chimed in. Once more, there was a calm peace in the room.

Havdalah was over. The girls were standing about chatting, when they noticed Bleemie walking over to the broken window. She carefully pulled out a large broken fragment. Both the students and teachers were surprised. "It's broken," they told her.

"I know. I want to hang this in my room at home."

It was hard to explain that this broken glass felt like a medal to her — a symbol of her people's perseverance through persecution. If she again became complacent in the luxury of America, she would look up at her wall and see her medal, see what it really meant to be a Jew. And she would remember that she had a responsibility to persecuted Jews wherever they might be.

"Now where's Rabbi Bleich? I've got an issue to be settled now." It was Sunday morning, bright and early, but already the teachers were up and about.

"The bed issue?" asked Tzippy with a giggle.

"Yup! And you're all in on this too. I need you for reinforcement."

All the teachers filed into Rabbi Bleich's tiny office and stood there in a semicircle. Rabbi Bleich looked up, "Uh, oh, looks like I'm in trouble."

"You might say that," agreed Brocha.

"How's it going over at the boys' school?"

"Fine, except that I need *tzitzis*. Now that I've taught them about it, we have to rotate the few pairs I have among the boys."

"Um, may I bring this conversation back on track?" asked Bleemie. "Consider the *tzitzis* a done deal. Of course they'll be shipped right away from America. You can't rotate *tzitzis*, right, Rabbi Bleich?"

"Right."

"That settles that issue. Next. Beds."

"Beds?"

"Somebody care to tell the good Rabbi what happened this Shabbos?"

Tzippy started giggling again. "Did you ever spend Friday night lying with your knees bent, on a kitchen floor, looking at the very dirty bottoms of a Russian kitchen cabinet."

"Can't say I did," chuckled Rabbi Bleich.

"Well, three of us now can boast of having done so."

"It's not as if we complained the week we did not have enough blankets and used our coats," broke in Brocha.

"And it's not as if we stopped having the Shabbos program the week there were no potatoes or flour, only lots and lots of carrots," said Tzippy.

"But we do need beds," said Bleemie in a tone that brooked no argument.

The story of their "Shabbos bedroom" had the desired results. Sunday afternoon the *shul* office purchased and delivered large futon mattresses. And so ended their problems. Every Shabbos, they would lay the mattresses across every square inch of floor, and the girls would be one big, happy family. It made Bleemie wonder just how many lice now had their homes in her hair!

⌒⌒

One cold Friday night, as the girls put on their coats before leaving *shul*, Bleemie noticed a little old man sitting sadly off to one side. All the married *shlichim*, who usually invited him for meals, had left for home.

Bleemie was familiar with this man. He was a homeless man, without any family, who would walk around the *shul* all week singing, *Keil Malei Rachamim...* He was the *Kaddish zugger,* both for his family members who had perished in the war, and for all the other Jews in Kiev who had no one to say *Kaddish* for them. Rabbi

Bleich had given him a bed in the boys' school to sleep in, but Shabbos could be very lonely in that building.

"*Gut Shabbos*," Bleemie said pleasantly. "Come, eat the Shabbos meal with us."

The man looked up and smiled gratefully.

Miriam materialized at Bleemie's side. Miriam had a heart of gold, always wanting to be included in a *mitzvah*. She handed the man his cane and helped him down the steps.

Bleemie and her students walked along slowly with the old man. When they reached the apartment, the girls trooped into the dining room, and Bleemie gave the old man a spot at the head of the table. Bleemie was no stranger to old homeless men. Her father specialized in gathering homeless souls and bringing them home for meals.

Bleemie went onto the porch to get the grape juice for *Kiddush*. She picked up the bottle and got a cascade of grape juice all over her dress. The bottom of the bottle had frozen off.

As she walked back in, she noticed Leah looking at her in a strange way. "Bleemie, can we talk?"

Bleemie looked down at the grape juice puddle forming at her feet, then nodded. "Sure."

"In there," said Leah, pointing to the kitchen.

Bleemie went into the kitchen. The other teachers followed and stood behind Leah. Bleemie, puzzled, looked at her friends, "What's the problem?"

"How could you invite him without asking us?" asked Chanie. "We run a girls' program. This isn't the place for a man like that."

"I don't understand," protested Bleemie. "Are you saying that we should have left him alone in *shul*?"

"The married *shlichim* should have taken care of him. He smells."

"I don't understand," said Bleemie a second time. She really did not understand. "You saw. The married *shlichim* were gone already."

"Well this is not just your program, Bleemie. We're in this together, and you should have asked us. None of us feels he should be here. I can't eat while he's here. He's gross."

"Look, we all have to do our bit. Mrs. Podolsky washes his

clothing. Her son, Shimon, who is younger than us, bathes him. And we should have left a *Yid* alone in *shul*, hungry and alone because *you* are grossed out?" Bleemie's voice caught, and she began to sob.

The teachers looked on in shock. This was out of character for Bleemie.

Bleemie put her head down on the counter and wept. She wept for the tragedy of this man's life, for the lost lives of his relatives and friends, for the moving prayers she had heard him intone.

Leah was taken aback. She began to suspect Bleemie of being on the verge of a nervous breakdown. How else to explain these heartwrenching sobs? She quickly put her arm around her friend. "It's okay he's here, Bleemie. Right, girls?" The other teachers voiced their quick assent.

"I'm fine. Please leave me alone."

The other girls left the kitchen, and Bleemie went on weeping. She wept for the fact that cruelty existed in the world, she wept for the punishment Hashem had wrought on His beloved children through the Holocaust, and she wept in the hopes that her own *tefillos* begging not to be cast away in her old age would find their way to the Heavenly throne.

Leah was really worried by Bleemie's reaction. She stole away from the dining room back into the kitchen. "Bleemie, it's okay," she said again.

Bleemie finally looked up and wiped her streaming eyes. "I couldn't help it, Leah; he breaks my heart."

"Mine too, Bleemie," said Leah. "I'm glad you brought him tonight. But we should make sure that every week another family takes him home."

Arm in arm, the two friends went back to the dining room to hear *Kiddush*. In the end, all were glad the old man had been their guest. He regaled the girls with stories of Kiev of old, described the various *minyanim* that had been Kiev's past glory, sang Yiddish songs for them, and kept the girls enthralled until the early hours of the morning. At night's end, Brocha, shamefaced, went over to her friend. "Bleemie," she said, "do you realize how much we all learned tonight about the power of giving to others?"

Bleemie nodded wordlessly. Then she handed the man his cane, and together with Miriam, walked her Shabbos guest "home" to the boys' school.

A Nostalgic Vision of Lost Glory
Interior of the Riga Synagogue

Chapter Twelve

∾ An "Americanske" in Kiev!

Regina's family had received the coveted American visa. Very soon they would be off to a new land, free from the hardships and anti-Semitism of Kiev.

Regina had a grandmother, for whom every *shaliach* in Kiev had a grudging admiration. She constantly ran after them, offering her services as a moneychanger, an occupation that was highly illegal. However, the best rates were always illegal. As much as she sometimes annoyed them, she always gave them a good rate. They also felt that they did a *mitzvah* every time they changed money through her, for this woman was ensuring that her family had American dollars for their move to America.

Every time Bleemie saw Regina's grandmother, she felt a twinge. This is what it used to be like to be Jewish for almost everyone. Living in conditions her great-grandparents had experienced, always worrying about tomorrow, the indomitable strength that she showed while being involved in these clandestine operations made this woman a study of the *Yiddishe babbeh*. She never allowed her children to do anything illegal, claiming that only she was old enough to risk imprisonment. And so she stood guard at the *shul*, stopping every foreigner, using her wits and her will to survive, to ensure the future for her son, his wife, and their daughter.

Regina's parents had invited the American teachers to their home countless times as a show of gratitude for their dollars. True, *Babushka* did not allow them to do the moneychanging; but at least they could thank them with warm hospitality.

The day finally came when Regina burst into the teachers' apartment in Podol, "We have our tickets already. We can leave in two weeks."

The teachers rejoiced with her, happy for her grandmother, knowing that it had been her perseverance that had paid off.

"My parents would like to take you on a tour of Kiev before we leave. They want to feel that they are giving something back to you," said Regina shyly.

The day of their sightseeing tour was bright and clear, although still a little cold. The girls strolled through the streets and museums, laughing, teasing, enjoying life as only Americans can — loudly. They didn't realize Regina's parents were embarrassed as their fellow Russians disapprovingly observed the spectacle.

"This was the winter palace of Catherine the Great," said Regina's father, leading the way to a castle of blue and gold on a bluff overlooking the Dnieper. Beautiful gardens and forests surrounded the castle like tissue paper nestled around a fragile gift. The girls wandered about, standing on stumps to make "revolutionary" speeches, acting like princesses and notables and in general making fools of themselves.

Refused entry to the castle, they sneaked in through a different door. Regina and her parents busily studied the potted plants. The girls got a mere halfway up the red, plush staircase, however, before the guard caught them and threw them out. Not forcibly, for they were "Americanske" and even he was a little in awe of them.

He smiled as they took pictures standing on the black, austere fence. Duty bound, he finally shooed them away and they drifted over to the building next door, the Russian Parliament. A large crowd was present 20 feet from the building standing behind police barriers. Some held placards, some just sat despondently, the ragtag demonstration committee asking for quicker change to their bitter lives. The girls snapped shots of them, then became bored with that too.

"I'm going into the Parliament," decided Brocha. She began to climb over the barrier, but the ripping sound from her skirt warned her to stop.

Malky noticed a guard staring curiously at their group, but didn't think anything of it — they had earned quite a number of stares today. She looked back to Brocha, who, lightheartedly, had decided to try getting under the bar. Bending down, she succeeded only in getting her head through to one side, while her torso remained on the other. Undeterred, she lay down and started inching her way under the barrier. The girls were laughing; but Regina and her parents were speechless with shock.

"*Stop! Stop! Stop!*" The screams, accompanied by the sound of boots pounding on the pavement, brought the girls' attention to a group of guards running towards them, hands on their guns.

"Brocha, quick," yelled Malky.

Leah panicked and jumped up and down for lack of something more constructive to do.

Brocha half under the bar, half out, was a little stuck and more than a little confused. "What? What's going on?" she asked Malky, who was looking at something right above her. Brocha lifted her eyes to meet the stare of a coterie of guards standing just above her.

"Uh, hello, I want to go in," explained Brocha from her prone position. The girls giggled, and the guards looked relieved. It was not some terrorist squad they were dealing with, just a bunch of crazy Americanskes.

"No allowed," said the guards, smiling good-naturedly. Brocha gave a wry grin of defeat. Inch by inch she extricated herself from under the bars.

Safely out of trouble, the girls turned to look for Regina and her parents. They saw them standing at a distance, pretending not to know them. It wasn't until the girls were out of sight of the Parliament that the family rejoined them. As a very anxious Regina parted from them, she asked, "In America, Bleemie, everyone is like you girls?"

That innocently worried question made the girls realize that it would not be easy for Regina to acclimate to America. Since Bleemie would be leaving not long after Regina, she was unanimously voted to be the one responsible for Regina's adjustment — not a task she thought herself quite capable of doing.

Perhaps the American girls could take a cue from Regina in extending the concepts of *tznius* and restraint into the realm of having fun. Perhaps, she reflected, as some of the afternoon's wilder scenes replayed themselves in her mind, there were things that she and her friends should learn from the Russian girls.

Chapter Thirteen

⟋ The Name Game

"While not all girls became observant, almost all took on a Jewish name. Some had been given names by previous *shlichim* in a haphazard fashion — "Your name is Lena so we'll call you Leah."

Rabbi Bleich did not agree with that method. He tried to impress upon the students and *shlichim* alike the importance of names. A name was more than just something to be called by. It was a prophecy for the future and a source of strength for the person.

Every student who wanted to take on a Jewish name thereafter had to do research into the name and learn about it. Rabbi Bleich's apartment was inundated with girls who wanted to research his book of names.

One girl could not make a decision. Weeks passed. She went to the Bleichs' apartment so frequently that the girls were sure that she had memorized the book. One day she finally came over to Bleemie to announce that she had decided on a name.

That Shabbos she stood proudly in *shul*, ready to be named officially during the Torah reading. There was a hushed silence as everybody waited to hear the result of her protracted reading. "So, *nu*, what's to be your name?" asked Rabbi Bleich.

"Yakova," said the girl proudly.

Poor Yakova. She never did quite live down the fact that it had taken her over a month to pick a name like Yakova.

Another student proudly took on the name Rochel. At a Shabbos *seudah,* Bleemie overheard her say, "Yeah, it was Chanie, but I like Rochel better."

Bleemie tried to sound casual. "What was Chanie?"

"My name before I named myself Rochel."

Bleemie felt her knees go weak. "Um, you mean some *shaliach* decided to call you Chanie, but you wanted the name Rochel?"

"No. When I was born, my grandmother gave me a name in *shul.*"

Bleemie just stood there staring dumbly. How was she to have supposed that a child in Russia had been given a Jewish name at birth?

"Well," she finally managed to say, "I think you are now blessed with *two* names, Chana Rochel!"

The significant thing about the name taking was that often the Jewish name did give the girl a certain strength. Take the example of the two little doves. Two best friends, sixth graders, took on the name "Yonah."

A few weeks after the naming, one girl's family decided to make *aliyah* within two weeks. She had been in the school barely two months, not enough to make her *Yiddishkeit* strong enough to last a lifetime.

Malky racked her brains for a way to make a lasting impact. Without asking permission, Malky took the liberty of pulling the two Yonahs from their secular classes and teaching them Jewish fundamentals instead. Their name became a theme: The Yonah of Shabbos, The Yonah trapped between two rocks, The Yonah symbolizing the Jews …

Two weeks passed by quickly, and Yonah V. left to Israel. It was not long before Malky received a long, chatty letter from her. She wrote that, being a Yonah, she had insisted on being put into a religious school. One Yonah had soared up in flight!

The Yonah left in Kiev had mostly irreligious friends. The pressures on her were enormous. One day she approached Malky.

"Malky, I have something to tell you."

"Yes?"

"After *shul* on Shabbos, I went to the theater." It was obvious that she felt guilty, and wanted to appease her conscience.

Malky was silent.

"My boyfriend took my ticket. I didn't carry or pay."

Malky remained silent, racking her brains for the right thing to say.

Yonah bent her head shyly. "I'll never do it again. It didn't feel right."

Smiling with relief, Malky tousled her student's hair. Some lessons were not needed. A Jewish soul can sometimes feel the truth. And another Yonah was soaring!

Chapter Fourteen

∞ Menorah Gets a Shot

Bleemie was by nature a meddlesome creature, prone to sticking her nose into other people's business. One Monday afternoon, she noticed a classroom full of noisy boys without a teacher. Although she was officially finished for the day, Bleemie retraced her steps to the principal's office.

"Esther, there is no teacher in the first-grade boys' classroom."

"I know, Bleemie," sighed Esther wearily. "I haven't had a teacher for them for the past week."

"That's terrible! I'm going in there to teach them." And with that, Bleemie marched back to the classroom.

She had picked the perfect day to undertake the project. Unknown to her, Rabbi Bleich had arranged for the Jewish television program, *Menorah*, to visit the school and film some classes.

Bleemie had barely managed to get the boys into their seats when the film crew walked in. She had not had a second to think about what she might teach these little boys. Now, here she was, stuck in front of the cameras.

First the little boys *davened*, then they *davened* some more. It was the only thing that their impromptu teacher was sure they knew how to do.

Bleemie walked around the classroom, pointing out the place, chanting with the boys. Alongside her walked a light man highlighting every facial blemish she had picked up in Russia, and a cameraman getting excellent sideshots of her long scraggly ponytail.

Then the film crew shot some footage of Bleemie teaching the boys about *Rosh Chodesh* in a smattering of broken Russian and Hebrew sentences. Dismissal time came none too early for Bleemie. With a prayer of thanks for the day's end, Bleemie skeddaddled from the school, anxious to put as much space between herself and the film crew.

A few hours later, Bleemie stood in the *shul*, taking care of arrangements for *Bnos Chayil*, the girls' youth group. As she was speaking to Edik, she noticed that he was becoming increasingly suave in his speech and mannerisms. He was smiling where no smiles were called for, gesticulating eloquently and glancing repeatedly towards the back of the room. Bleemie turned around to see the *Menorah* group getting the back view of her ponytail that they had missed in the classroom. This time she was trapped. She graciously answered their questions, smiling at the camera, trying to help Russians understand why the Americans came to Kiev.

"So you came to Kiev to be Mary Moviestar," Malky teased when she came in and saw her friend's entourage. Bleemie's smile took a somewhat sinister twist as she turned to the cameraman. "That girl is really one of the best teachers here," she said, pointing at Malky. "She even gives classes for the Russian teachers."

Suddenly, the bright light switched to Malky's face, the cameraman was practically up her nose, and a polite Russian interviewer began grilling Malky. Blinking in the darkening room, Bleemie fled from the *shul* to the safety of her apartment.

Purim was on the way! A concert was planned for all the Jews of Kiev. Simcha Weber, the singing sensation from America, was arriving on *Taanis Esther*.

On the fast day, there was no school. Instead, the girls came to the *shul* to bake *hamantashen*. While the little cakes were baking, two

A Bnos Chayil Group in Kiev

girls at a time were taken to Bleemie's apartment, where cartons of gently used clothing from America sat waiting. Each girl was given a chance to choose two outfits.

"Ooh, can I have this top?" asked Inna, picking up a black-and-white sweater from the back of a chair.

"Sure," said Bleemie.

"But that's *your* sweater she just asked you about," hissed Malky into her friend's ear.

"I don't care about these clothes anymore, Malky. I'm leaving soon. Let her have it."

By nightfall the girls were ready to go to the concert, the apartment was a muddle of boxes, string, and torn bags, Bleemie had two outfits left to her name, and they were into the spirit of Purim full swing.

The concert was magnificent. Three thousand Russian Jews shouted "Amein!" to the *brachos*, heard the Megillah together, then enjoyed Simcha Weber's beautiful voice and heartfelt songs. In the aisles, souls ablaze, the Jews of Kiev danced a Purim rikud.

The next day, there was a smaller Purim event, just for the school's students and families. It took a while for the students to

Preparing for Purim

recognize their teachers underneath the varied and ridiculous costumes they had devised. Bleemie had a stocking on her head and was dressed as a scarecrow. "Only Bleemie would put a stocking over her head," was the general consensus of opinion. There was food, music, and good cheer in abundance. Leaving the dance circle in an effort to catch her breath, Bleemie found herself standing near Tanya's grandmother.

"Bleemie, for what you have done for our Tanya, we can't thank you enough," said the woman.

"She's doing so well, isn't she?" asked Bleemie.

"You know, this is the first year we see her smiling, laughing, having a good time." There were tears in the elderly woman's eyes as she remembered the hard times that the child had endured.

"*Slava Boga* — thank G-d!" said Bleemie simply.

Tanya's grandmother leaned forward to Bleemie earnestly. "Take her with you to America. Please, Bleemie."

Bleemie was taken aback. Take her where? How? In her suitcase? The smile faded from her face as she searched for a way to explain that it was an impossible request.

"She has no future here, Bleemie. I beg of you, take her."

Bleemie looked at the dance floor, where Tanya was whirling

around. She looked back at the pleading eyes of the old woman. Then, taking a deep breath, Bleemie made a promise she did not know how she would live up to. "I'll do everything in my power to get her to America."

Miriam's grandmother, standing directly behind them, had heard the conversation. Now she tapped Bleemie on the shoulder. "My granddaughter, too," she begged.

Bleemie blanched.

Miriam's grandmother began to cry. "We don't even have enough food to give her, Bleemie. Even if we never see her again, as long as we know she is being taken care of, as long as we know she has a chance for a decent life —" Miriam's grandmother bent her head and sobbed heartbrokenly.

Bleemie attempted to stem her own tears, to no avail. Two wet streaks appeared on the stocking that still covered her head. "Where are you, American *Kehillah*?" Bleemie heard voices in her head cry out. "You're dancing for joy this Purim, giving elaborate *shalach manos*, eating lavish *seudos* — Think of these kids. Isn't Purim about unity and love betwen the members of the Jewish community?"

Bleemie choked back a sob, then turned decisively towards Miriam's grandmother. "I don't know what I can possibly accomplish, but whatever I can do to get these girls to America, I will do!"

A more sober Bleemie rejoined the dance circle. She had a lot to think about and plan for.

At the party's end, the teachers made their way out of the hall. Bleemie was suddenly blinded by high-powered halogen lights. Once again, there were cameras in her face. Bleemie smiled, and her stocking-covered head shifted to a rakish angle. "Let them film away," she thought, "no one will have any inkling that the idiot underneath this sweaty stocking is me!"

Wrong again, Bleemie. She couldn't believe her ears — the interviewer was saying, "And this is the teacher whom we filmed a few days ago in the Jewish school."

Bleemie put her straw hat over her face and fled.

" Anyone who wants 'pull' in Heaven should get involved in Russian Kiruv…" — Rabbi Yaakov Kamenetsky.

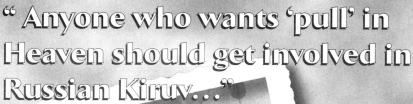

Rabbi Nosson Sherman, General Editor of Artscroll/Mesorah Publications speaking at the Kiev School Graduation Ceremony. Rabbi Bleich is translating into Russian.

A Graduation Ceremony

The Proud Students

Kapporas

A Pidyon Haben

Thirteen Campers cekebrated their Pidyon Haben, traditionally done by a father when his first-born son is 30 days old. These boys' fathers however, did not know to do so — and the sons redeemed themselves after learning the Dinim.

A Decorated Sukkah

Benching Lulav and Esrog, Kiev

A Meal in the Sukkah

Preparing for Sukkos!
Above, Rabbi M. Finkel decorates a Sukkah.

Clouds
of
Glory

Part Two

Chapter Fifteen

∞ The Return

As a farewell trip three days before Bleemie would leave to America, the teachers planned to go sightseeing to all the surrounding places of Jewish interest. On Sunday morning they awoke early and waited for their driver. An hour passed, then another and yet another, but the driver never showed up.

The other teachers decided to go shopping, and Bleemie, bored with the inactivity, began to pack. She dragged out a suitcase and removed her passport and ticket from the side pocket. She flipped her ticket open, and her eyes widened in disbelief. Once again, the *Ananei HaKavod* were apparent.

Her flight was due to leave Moscow the next evening! And she would have to get a train soon to be there on time! Baruch Hashem the driver had been unreliable! Bleemie took her ticket and ran to the *shul* to find Rabbi Bleich.

She barged into his office, barely waiting for his response to her curt knock.

"Rabbi Bleich," she gasped, "this is an emergency! I must get to Moscow!"

The rabbi, used to Bleemie's emergencies, didn't even blink.

"What are you talking about? Aren't you supposed to be in Berditchev now?"

"Yes, but the driver didn't show — and it's a real *mazal* he didn't. I have to get to Moscow."

"Why?"

"You won't believe it, but I made a mistake. My flight is leaving tomorrow night."

"What? You're right! I almost *don't* believe it." Rabbi Bleich looked at his watch and consulted a schedule which he pulled out of his desk drawer. "You have two hours to pack. I'll send Igor to pick you up. Be in touch when you arrive in America and have a safe trip!"

Clutching her ticket, Bleemie flew down the steps of the *shul* and through the streets of Kiev. She threw what was left of her belongings into her suitcase, put that one into the now-empty larger one, and wrote goodbye letters to the other teachers and *shlichim*. The hardest part was writing to her precious students.

Her time in Kiev had come full circle. Igor had met her at the airport on her arrival. Now he was seeing her off. Her bags, to his great relief, were considerably lighter this time. He walked her onto the train and stowed her baggage in the compartment. "Now I want you to lock the door behind me and don't come out until you get to Moscow," he ordered in a voice of authority.

Bleemie did as she was bidden and leaned against the door. She looked around the small compartment, two beds on either side of her and a small pull-out table beneath the train window. As she glanced about, the biggest cockroach she had ever seen paraded across the bed. She glanced at the other bunk. One could barely see the cover through the swarming brown bugs. Bleemie shuddered, knowing full well that for the next 12 hours she was stuck in this small space with these cockroaches. She buttoned up her coat, put her hat low on her forehead and, her skin crawling, lay down in a fetal position on her suitcase.

The train clacked its way steadily through the Russian country side. Scenes of scattered rural areas would remain forever in Bleemie's mind, split-second sights of old Russian peasants working with out-dated rickety tools, hacking at the ground with rusty metal picks, following behind horse-drawn plows. She passed homes that looked as if they were hanging on by virtue of splinters of wood and clods of dried mud alone, saw the countryside that she had read about so many times, the gulag scene.

Moscow. The train slowed down as it neared the station, hissing as it lost speed. Once again, she was picked up by a Moscow-based *shaliach*. Being escorted to the airport, boarding the plane, settling in her seat — Bleemie felt as if she were in the last frame of a movie that she didn't want to see end. The curtain on her Russian teaching experience was descending.

"Miss —" The stewardess was bending over her."We have a slight problem. The husband of the woman next to you wants to sit near her. We will give you a seat in first class, if you would please give him this seat."

"No problem." Bleemie would have been happy to accommodate the couple without the bribe, but now didn't seem the time to mention it.

The stewardess led her to a seat right next to an elaborately coiffed, well-dressed woman. Bleemie settled gratefully into the large, cushioned chair, reflecting that she had anticipated a slow adjustment to simple luxuries like abundant toilet paper. And here she was, thrown right into the unaccustomed, but welcome, lap of luxury.

All 15 members of the Kleiner family stood waiting for Bleemie. Next to them stood an obviously assimilated Jew, holding his small son. He was trying not to stare, but the tumult and excitement generated by the Kleiners kept drawing his attention to them. It was fascinating to watch such a large close-knit family, and he felt an urge to find out more about them.

"Who are you waiting for?"

"For my sister," little Mirel piped up proudly.

"You mean there is another one of you?" he asked incredulously.

All the Kleiners laughed knowingly and nodded.

"And you can actually tell that she's missing."

His question only made them laugh harder. Miss their harum-scarum Bleemie? Who wouldn't?

As the plane winged its way to America, Bleemie had much to think about. Next to her, the well-dressed woman was on her sixth drink, steadily getting drunk. Bleemie felt sorry for her. What did she have, this wealthy woman? She obviously had no idea of the beauty of Torah. What riches could she have accumulated to compare with the riches of having students who were *frum* because of what you taught them?

As the plane winged its way to America, Bleemie had much to think about. Next to her, the well-dressed woman was on her sixth drink, steadily getting drunk. Bleemie felt sorry for her. What did she have, this wealthy woman? She obviously had no idea of the beauty of Torah. What riches could she have accumulated to compare with the riches of having students who were *frum* because of what you taught them?

The man held his little son's hand and walked over to Mr. Kleiner. "Excuse me, but you look so happy. Your family looks so close. What is your secret?"

"There is no secret. We live according to G-d's Laws. There is no other prescription for happiness."

The man grimaced. He had hoped for some realistic advice, not some fanaticism.

"And for whom are you waiting?" asked Mr. Kleiner politely.

"My wife was away on a business trip."

"Oh!"

There was an awkward silence between the two men, then both turned to watch the arrival screen again.

Bleemie stepped off the plane and stood in line in front of the customs window, still in a daze. She had finally fallen asleep for the last two hours of the flight.

"Welcome back to the United States," said the official as he waved her through. That made it real for her. She was really back in America.

Through the swinging doors she went, dragging her suitcase whose wheels had not survived their maiden voyage, her Russian hat perched over her overgrown hair. There they were, the whole kit and caboodle, arms outstretched and eyes shining! Her seatmate walked over to the man near the Kleiners and pecked the man and the boy on their cheeks. Bleemie wondered fleetingly if her husband could smell the alcohol on his wife's breath. Then, shaking her head at such a waste of a life, Bleemie turned back to her beloved family.

The family all realized something had changed in their happy-go-lucky Bleemie. She was fired with a purpose.

Her students had to come to America. There were no two ways about it and she would not take no for an answer. Kosher food had to be sent to Russia, along with *sefarim*, medicine and clothing. There was so much to do.

The family had laughed when they saw Bleemie pull the broken pane from the *shul* window out of her suitcase, but they all soon came to respect that bit of glass for what it represented to her. Whoever teased her was sure to hear the quote from Rav Yaakov Kamenetzky, "Anyone who wants 'pull' in Heaven should get involved in Russian *Kiruv*." It was a line that forestalled any discussions about her relaxing. She had gone to Kiev an ordinary complacent American teenager and had come back a dedicated *Bas Yisrael*.

The bottom line!
Yad Yisroel Girls' Camp, Ukraine, 1998

Chapter Sixteen

∞ Written With Love

Tanya walked into the school building on Monday morning and was surprised to see a huddle of girls standing at the bulletin board, staring as if in shock. Then she saw Miriam, head against the wall, crying.

Tanya walked over to the group and made her way to the front of the bulletin board. A big bright oaktag hung at a rakish angle. In multicolored magic markers, interspersed with smiley faces and hearts, was written:

"Dear Girls, WRITE, WRITE, WRITE. The following is my address and I expect you to use it. I love you all and will miss you all. I'm sorry we couldn't say goodbye face to face, but my flight left unexpectedly yesterday. Make me proud, girls. I love you and hope to see you all soon in America or in Israel. With all my love, with hugs and kisses, Bleemie."

Tanya felt a sob catch in her throat. She tilted her head back in a vain effort to stop the tears from falling, then ran to her classroom to the solitude of her desk.

Dear Bleemie,

How are you? In Shabbos without you was lot of sadness (not sadness because of Shabbos, but because you is absent). Now, Rochel continues our lessons. With her we learn a book, 19 Letters wich was written by Rabi Hirsh. Now I'm preparin for Pesach and its very difficult. Two new girls our class entered. They love our school and one of them came to Shabbos once.
Happy Pesach.
Don't be sad.

 I miss you.
 Love Miriam

My dearest teacher and sister, Bleemie

I and everybody real miss our Bleemie. Every Shabbos we remember you when we all together. All Bnos D'Kiev was very obsurd when you lefted us. Oh! I forget, on TV last week was program Menorah and they show you there so you so popular here. I have not more news.
Please write me.

 I love you!
 Avigayil

Dear Bleemie,

Thank you for the letter. I celebrated holydays with Bashy and girls from my school. You asked about anything I need. If you can buy books about Judaism, about religion with Russian translation. I think that's all I need now.
Please don't forget me.
Kiss you.

 With love,
 Olga

Dear Bleemie

I don't have telephone. Thank you for your lessons and beautiful present. I very glad what I know you. I so sorry you go away. Write a letter or give me a cold.

 Bye.
I hope see you again.

Every day, Bleemie would stand at the mailbox, waiting for that day's missives. Her students never missed a day. Little Russian envelopes stuffed with their heartfelt lines, crayon drawings and even stickers kept Bleemie in touch with "her" girls.

After every letter, Bleemie would cry. She knew that her family could not understand why she was such an emotional mess. The only person who could understand was someone who had been there, had been part of the "Kiev" experience.

Tzippy became her lifeline.

"Tzippy, I can't stand it. I miss Russia. I want to go back."

"My parents would tie me up if I said I was going back."

"Mine too. Tzippy, we've got to get the girls here. We've got to!"

Bleemie plunged into the work of finding schools to accept her students. Once accepted in an American school, they would be entitled to student visas and could be on their way to her.

Bleemie had read so much about the rescue operations that were undertaken in World War II that she naively thought that all high school would be eager to accept her students. After all, most of the American *mosdos* were set up and directed by war survivors who surely understood the importance of bringing these Jewish souls out of the Communist wasteland. She was devastated to find that no one was willing to accept them.

In desperation, she turned to her own alma mater, the Bais Yaakov she had attended, and asked them to accept Tanya. As she sat confidently across the desk from her former principal, she imagined how he would express his pride at getting involved in this essential *kiruv* work.

He could not meet her eyes. "You understand, Bleemie? I can't accept Russians."

Bleemie stared at him in disbelief. She felt like crying out, "But you were a Lithuanian when you got here. You too were a foreigner. My mother was a Hungarian —" But all she could manage was a feeble, "Why not?"

"I can't risk our girls."

"But it isn't a risk. She's *frum*. Even more religious than I am!"

"I feel badly, but I just can't accept her. Why don't you try other schools?"

"That's what everyone says! 'Try a different school — not mine.' At what point will a school say, 'Yes, this is what schools are meant for'?"

"I feel badly, but you do understand, no?" He fingered his pen, still unable to look her in the face.

No! No! NO! She *didn't* understand. Nor did she want to understand that all the lessons she had learned had merely been lip service. What was the use of all the *Yahadus* that was taught, if it was not applied?

"Bleemie, you know there are schools for such girls, schools set up especially for Russians."

Why? Why should they be put into separate schools? These girls had worked harder at their *Yiddishkeit* than anyone she knew, had spent hours studying to bring themselves up to a Bais Yaakov level and no school would accept them. She had never expected anything like this from people she'd always respected.

Bleemie was almost at the end of her patience and stamina when she called Bais Rochel of Monsey.

"Impressive. We would be delighted to have Tanya join our school."

Bleemie was overjoyed! She'd found a school that lived up to the ideals it taught!

Bais Yaakov of Boro Park, Sara Schenirer Seminary, Breuer's Teachers Seminary, Bais Yaakov Academy and Yeshiva of Brooklyn also accepted her students. Her faith in the *chinuch* system was restored as she found schools who believed they were there to teach any Jewish child who wanted to learn.

With schools to attend and their papers in order, her girls would soon be on their way. The first two to be arriving would be Tanya and Miriam. Avigayil and Regina were already here, having arrived "legally" with their families.

Bleemie excitedly sent letters of the good news to Kiev. It didn't take too long for the reply to come back.

Dearest Bleemie

Hi! It was very nice to get your letter. I have many questions to you after it. R' Yankel told me I study in school in Monsey. But I don't know what kind of seminary and how long I shall study there. Please write me about family I have to live. I don't think all my papers will be finished in beginning of August.

Write me back.

Love Tanya

Chapter Seventeen

∞ Let All Those Who Are Hungry Come and Eat

Bleemie had told her family countless times of the food shortages in Russia, but they still were shocked when Avigayil came to visit. Little Rechy, too young to be tactful, blurted out, "She just ate a whole chicken!"

"Where did she put it?" wondered Tzirel aloud. It was a legitimate question. Where did the small-framed skinny girl manage to put all that food? Other people were harder to convince. The most common statement that Bleemie heard was, "How can you tell me there's no food in Russia? All the Russians I see are fat!" It took all her self-control to patiently repeat that Russians ate mostly starch and little else. Almost every teacher had gained weight in Russia.

What shocked Bleemie beyond words was the fact that it seemed to be very difficult to convince people of the significance of the cause and the direness of the need of the people in Kiev.

Time and time again, Bleemie was to experience rejection and disinterest. A lesser person than she might have become disillusioned or discouraged — but not our Bleemie.

The memory of those beautiful souls that she had left behind in Kiev energized her to exercise continued, persistent action.

Every time Bleemie closed her eyes, she would hear the pleas of Miriam's grandmother. "She has no future here. We have no food to give her. Please, take her, take the child, so she can live."

Then scenes of the time she had watched the Chabad airlift would also flash in her mind. Eighty children were being taken to Israel. Eighty pairs of excited, frightened eyes looked out of the windows of the bus that would take them to the airport. The fathers, mothers and grandparents ran after the bus, waving handkerchiefs, blowing kisses. The tears that followed once the bus was out of view were bittersweet, signifying a mixture of loss and hope. Many of these families had told Bleemie at that time, "It is hard for me to send my child, but he's better off where he'll be fed."

Yad Yisroel began a food campaign, "Cans for Kiev," and Bleemie's faith in the American community was renewed. Children of all ages brought cans and quarters to school. Container after container of food was soon being shipped to Kiev. Bleemie loved going into the warehouse where the food was being stored, to look for renewed encouragement in the stacks and stacks of food that had been collected.

Chol Hamoed Succos, Grades 1-3 visiting the shul and succah in Kiev, 1997
We never know just how far our tzedakah dollars go!

Girls' Camp, Ukraine, 1998

Bleemie drafted her sisters to collect money for the Kiev community. During the worst snowstorm in memory, the girls gathered their hand-painted oaktag signs and a large *pushka*, and off they went collecting. Their target was a popular grocery where there were sure to be hundreds of people coming and going, even on a day like today. The girls were quite a sight with their bundled up attire, their arms straight out, their bodies and signs attracting the thick heavy flakes that soon transformed them into snow sculptures. Every person who passed dropped some money in the *pushka*. "I wonder — is it because they believe in our cause," mused Rechy, "or because they feel sorry for us standing out here in the snow?" She stamped her feet vigorously.

"Whichever one," shrugged Laya, "as long as we manage to raise money."

An elderly man stopped on his way out of the grocery store, a shopping bag swinging from his hand. As he passed the girls, he stopped to see what they were doing. He brushed away the snow that clung to their hand-lettered signs and read to himself, his lips moving softly. Nodding to himself, as if in agreement with the words on the sign, he pulled a dollar bill out of his pocket and deposited it in the *pushka*.

"Good luck," he called out with a smile, as he turned towards his car.

Suddenly he paused and turned back to the girls. Clearing his throat a few times, a nostalgic smile on his face, he said, "You know, you girls remind me of what I did years ago. The Joint sent us kids out to collect money to save the Jews of Europe during World War II. My friends and I would station ourselves with tablecloths on street corners and in front of stores. We would call out to everybody to help the Joint save lives. And we felt really good, when at the end of the day, we joined the corners of the tablecloth together on a heap of money. We knew we were doing something important."

The girls smiled, then Laya said quietly, "Sir, I just want you to know you are looking at the outcome of your money."

The man looked at her quizzically.

"My parents are holocaust survivors. They've told us over and over how the food from the Joint kept them going. What you collected is what kept my parents alive. So I suppose you are one of those to be thanked for the fact that I exist."

The man peeled out another dollar bill from his wallet and wordlessly added it to the collection can.

From the U.S. to Russia,
dollars that really count!

Chapter Eighteen

∞ Time for a Reality Check

Regina had been accepted in Bais Yaakov of Boro Park. Surprisingly, she was pretty much on par with her class mates scholastically, but Bleemie felt that Regina still lacked American social skills. Once a week Bleemie would tutor her, spending hours coaching her on the finer points of taste and behavior. She also made sure to "lighten" up the lessons with trips to amusement parks and the like.

There were some concepts that Regina still could not grasp. "I don't understand. Why do blue and green, red and purple, orange and pink not match and yet the dressmakers can put it together? I'll never get this matching business. I guess I'll always look different."

Bleemie reached over and hugged her. "C'mon, I bet you'll have it down pat in two weeks. Not a day more. Now for some fun. This is Coney Island. Pick any ride you want to go on."

Regina tilted her head and looked from dizzying ride to dizzying ride. "That one," she said pointing at the roller coaster.

Oh no! Bleemie was always amazed at how she got herself into these situations. What self-destructive force allowed her to offer to go on any ride that a 15-year-old would pick out? She gritted her teeth and made her way to the line for the roller coaster.

Bleemie didn't remember much of the ride, other than the pain of her neck snapping back and forth like a limp rag doll's, and the imprint of her fingers on Regina's wrist.

At last the ride was over, and Bleemie gratefully climbed out. Taking a deep breath and trying to look as nonchalant as possible under the circumstances, she turned to Regina and, ever asking for punishment, asked, "Which ride next?"

"That one," said Regina pointing to the ferris wheel.

Bleemie felt herself turning green as she stepped into the little car. Her fear of heights was legendary in her family, but how was Regina to know? The ferris wheel started up, and Bleemie tried to keep her eyes fixed on her hands, not looking out, proud of keeping her cool in such an adverse situation.

The ferris wheel did a couple of rounds, then stopped, with their car at the topmost position. Their car swayed back and forth gently, waiting for the ride to resume. A frightened glance out the window set Bleemie off. She felt the tears begin and hastily started saying *Tehillim*.

"I want to go home," she whimpered, her pride totally gone.

"So do I," replied her student in an equally quavery voice.

Once down on the safe, blessed ground, Bleemie turned to Regina. "Any game you want to play is fine with me. But I've had it with rides!"

That night, as Bleemie recounted the tale, her parents looked at one another in that special way that Bleemie knew meant trouble. That look was usually the prelude to a discussion that she'd rather not be part of.

"We've been meaning to talk to you," said her mother.

Bleemie tried not to sound too defensive. "Why? What's up?"

"We're very proud of what you are doing, Bleemie; but we think it's time you started looking for a job here in America, instead of just floating through your life volunteering."

"Can't I just go back to Kiev?"

"Bleemie, time for a reality check. You've got to think about what you need to do, not just what you want to do."

"You think they don't need me to teach in Kiev."

"They might need teachers in Kiev," her father agreed.

COMMITTED TEACHERS NEEDED!
Baking and learning (cakes and challah) simultaneously in Camp Yad Yisroel, Ukraine

For a split second, Bleemie saw herself back on an airplane, bags loaded with supplies, returning to her beloved students.

"But someone else," he added firmly, "will have to go for now. Your job in life is to be a mother, *im Yirtzeh Hashem*. It's time to think of *shidduchim*, of settling down, taking responsibility for your own life too. *Chayecha kodmim*."

"Do you mean you're really not going to let me go back to teach in Russia?" Bleemie sounded incredulous.

"Bleemie —"

"I know, I know. But who wants a dumb job, anyway."

"So don't get a dumb job. Get a smart one."

"Actually," Bleemie conceded, "they need a temp at the Agudah for the next four months to work on their dinner. Is that acceptable? And then after that time, if I haven't found my *basherte*, can we renegotiate about going back to teach in Kiev?"

"You can temp for the next four months, but, you will keep dating until such time as you do find your *basherte*. End of discussion. No renegotiation."

Bleemie shot an appealing glance at her mother, who seemed to have steeled herself for just such a look and shook her head firmly.

Teaching again in Kiev was not going to be a part of her future. At least she had not yet saddled herself with a full-time job commitment. And who knew, maybe, just maybe, somehow, someway, her parents would rethink their decision and allow her to return to Kiev after the four months were up!

It's so hard to say good-bye!
Camp Yad Yisroel, girls' division

Chapter Nineteen

∽ Malky Goes Back

Malky, too, had not been able to tear herself away from Russia for too long. Although most of the girls wanted to go back, Malky was the only one whose parents allowed her to go. She would be teaching in the school in Vinitsa.

After three months, her mother decided on a reality check too, and Malky came back to America, via Kiev. Bleemie begged her for an eye-witness report of her students. Malky gave her a rundown of all the programs, as well as an update on all the girls.

Towards the end of the conversation, Malky asked hesitantly, almost apologetically, "Did you hear about Olga?"

"No. How is she doing in Netanya?" asked Bleemie.

"She's not in Netanya."

"She's not?! Where is she then?"

"Still in Kiev. She's engaged to a *goy*."

"WHAT?!?!"

"I still can't believe it either, Bleemie, but Shifra says it's true."

Shifra was Olga's best friend, so she would know, yet the news was incomprehensible to Bleemie. "It can't be!" she protested.

"That's what I thought — but *nebach* it is true."

Olga! Her Jewish-looking, Jewish-feeling Olga, the one who loved Jewish history — who said she'd marry only someone who shared that same history! She had to write immediately and try to prevent this tragedy from stealing her Olga away from the Jewish nation.

> Dearest Olga,
>
> Sorry this letter is not on nice stationery. I wanted to write to you right away when I heard where you are and what you are doing.
>
> I was sure you were in Israel — perhaps in nursing school. I wrote a letter asking for your address but never got it. And now I'm told you're still in Russia. Why didn't you write and tell me?
>
> I heard a rumor — I can't believe it and I hope it is not true. Somebody said you are dating a non-Jew. Olga, knowing you, I decided it cannot be true — but, Olga, I know how hard life is in Russia and how hard it is to stick to your beliefs when faced with choices. I am therefore writing you to be mechazek you, strengthen you and hopefully be proud of you.
>
> I'm sorry now that my Russian is not good enough so that I could write in your language
>
> "Words that come from the heart enter the heart," which means if you really mean what is said, the person listening will understand — even in a different language. Olga, this letter comes from my heart. I hope it touches yours.
>
> Olga, do you remember the Jewish history lessons? You are a part of a nation that has been through such hard times and yet always stuck to its beliefs. Your great-great-great-grandparents and mine went through all kinds of tortures — progroms, Hitler — and yet they stayed strong, kept the Torah, married Jews, so that you, Olga, would be born Jewish with the ability to rise spiritually. I think of us two as part of a golden chain stretching all the way back to Avraham Avinu. Through your grandparents' efforts, you were born, a golden link to a past. Don't you want your children to be golden links too? Don't you want them to feel a connection to your great-grandparents — to your past?
>
> When I came to Russia I said, "How beautiful it is to be a Jew," because no matter where in the world you go, you are never alone. You are a part of the family of Jews. My Russian students and friends are my relatives because they are Jewish — just as a

Chinese Jew would be my relative. I am a part of a whole, a member of a nation. Don't remove yourself from this whole, Olga.

Do you remember how you cried when we said, "Goodbye"? I cried the whole of last night, Olga, and am crying as I write this letter — because I'm scared you're going to say, "Goodbye," to being my fellow Jew.

There is a little girl in the Hebrew school in Kiev whose father is not Jewish and her mother is Jewish. The little girl is Jewish according to Jewish law. BUT I wish you could see as I did how hard her life is emotionally. Her father got angry at her for wanting to keep Shabbos and told her, "If you keep your Shabbos, I will keep mine." Imagine, father and daughter have different Shabbosim. The girl was ashamed because her father did not have a "bris"; but he didn't have to — he was not Jewish. Father and daughter did not share the same past and were not part of the same whole!

Olga, if there is anything I can do to help you through these hard times, let me know. Maybe you would like to come to America? Don't be shy — tell me how I can help you be strong and shine like the jewel you are. My thoughts and heart are with you, Olga, and I know you'll make the right decision — because after all you're the great Olga I remember.

With all my love
and hoping to hear from you,
Bleemie

No reply was forthcoming from Kiev.

A short while later Bleemie attended a *Melaveh Malkah* for former counselors and teachers of the Kiev *Mosdos*. As she sat there, a snatch of conversation from a nearby table wafted her way.

"… and I told my father that Rabbi Bleich should not bring out any more girls until there is a better program set up for them."

Bleemie turned abruptly to see who had come up with that gem. The speaker was the daughter of one of the well-known *g'virim* in America. Bleemie had encouraged her to be a counselor in *Machane Shuva* in Kiev. The two months she had spent there had obviously convinced her that she was now an expert on Russian Jews and their plight.

While the girl did spend time helping Russian girls enter her community to acclimate, she would often berate the people who brought those girls to America. Usually able to ignore her, Bleemie felt a flash of anger coursing through her. She pushed her chair away from the table with a loud scrape.

"And who are you to talk?" Bleemie lashed out. She knew her temper was out of control, but she could no longer put up with people looking for excuses to shrug off their nonparticipation. "Your father gave you every luxury a girl could ever want or need — and you are ready to condemn these Jewish girls to assimilated lives without proper medical attention, with minimum food?"

The girl looked at Bleemie abashed. "They're used to that food. It's not so bad for them."

"You can't imagine what you sound like! You sound like everything that makes the American Jewish community look selfish and uncaring. Because they are used to their hair falling out from Chernobyl, because they are used to dying of standard strep, therefore they should be satisfied with staying that way for years until we can make everything perfect for them here?"

The girl's eyes filled with tears and Bleemie wanted to bite off her tongue. She regretted the temper that had unleashed the harsh words.

But these were her girls they were talking about — her students who needed the acceptance of the American Jewish community, needed visas, schools and host families. Attitudes such as this girl's were not helpful. Bleemie managed to soften her voice somewhat before going on, yet an undercurrent of anger still was apparent.

"Chedva, the Hungarians had a German Rav, the Chasam Sofer, who revitalized their *Yiddishkeit*. Years later, the Germans got a Hungarian Rav, Rav Breuer, who revitalized *their* community. You know the saying, *'Galgal chozeir'*? There is a turning wheel!

"Did you hear what Rabbi Bleich said at the convention? When the Russians came to America at the turn of the century and tried to establish yeshivos, the Americans smiled and said, 'What do you think this is — Russia?' When he went to Russia now to establish yeshivos, the Russians smiled and said, 'What do you think this is — America?' "

By this time, all talk had ceased in the hall and everyone was openly eavesdropping. Bleemie could not care less. Let more girls receive an education.

"Now you're the 'rich American.' It's a responsibility. Did you ever wonder why Hashem brought your grandparents here to America? Why He saved them from the Holocaust?

"There's a reason why you ended up here and others ended up stuck behind the Iron Curtain. You were assigned the role of giving. You won't? Fine. But then when the wheel turns, what will your descendants deserve?"

Bleemie's voice cracked. She knew she would start crying before her tirade was over, but she couldn't stop. She had to get it out of her system.

"You know, I always wondered — when the Cantonists, innocent Jewish boys, were snatched from their homes and way of life — what happened to the people who were silent? But we know what happened — their children were snatched by the Communists and lost to us. When the wheel turns, Chedva, *chas v'shalom* that someone would say that the Jewish community shouldn't help your descendants. The world revolves around *midah k'neged midah*, and no one escapes the exacting justice of *Din*."

Chedva was crying softly. Bleemie was crying too. She had not meant to be that harsh. She knew that the girl did help out, but the memory of Olga was still branded on her heart. The guilty thought that if they had brought her to America, she would still be *frum*, was too fresh to allow Bleemie to judge Chedva favorably.

And yet — this is what it's all about!

Chapter Twenty

∞ A Working Girl Now

Multicolored posters lined the Kleiners' kitchen floor. Bleemie gazed mournfully at the signs she had completed. "Unartistic people should never attempt to teach elementary school," she announced. "I think I'll give this up for a while and call Malky."

"Why not give it up entirely?" suggested her sister Laya. "Let Regina do it. She's artistic."

"Good thinking, sis. Now, I can shmooze with Malky without a shred of guilt."

Bleemie picked up the phone.

"Hi, Malky, 'tis but me, Bleemie. Did you know that as of tomorrow I will be a working girl — not just a temp working girl, but a bona fide employee with a job responsibility?"

"Good for you. Welcome back to reality. What kind of job?"

"Teaching. Russian boys, at the Yeshiva Academy."

"Boys?!" Malky's voice boomed through loud and clear.

Bleemie grimaced and held the receiver away from her ear.

"Now why would you want to teach boys?"

"What does want have to do with it? Even idealists need jobs. It really beats bouncing around from one temp job to another."

"But boys? How will you ever control them?"

"You make it sound as if I'll be teaching high school. Fourth graders are still little kids. It won't be that hard."

"Don't come crying to me."

"I won't, if you stop *kvetching* to me how pointless you find your office job."

"Touché. Call me if you need help."

"I'll be calling you often, you can be sure. Do you know how orange juice sometimes comes in concentrate, all condensed —"

"Oh no, tell me you will not give me some goofy Bleemie philosophy!"

Bleemie blithely ignored the pointed insult. "Well, friendships made in Kiev are a lot like that — concentrated friendships. Essence packed into the small time we spent together."

"Bleemie, honey, don't ever try philosophy as a career."

"I won't. I'm a confirmed teacher now. Look, there are things we do for money, like your office job. Then we do things to make life fulfilling, like helping friends like me teaching fourth-grade boys."

"But you know Yeshiva Academy is full of Bukharians. Working with them is a whole different ball game than working with kids from Kiev."

"A Jew is a Jew is a Jew."

"Yah, but Jews do speak different languages at times — and have different cultures."

"But the Torah we share is the same."

"You'll call next week to let me know how you're managing?"

"If not sooner! I'd better get my posters off the floor before someone steps on them. Speak to you soon."

⤙⤚

"Hello, my name is Morah Kleiner." It was Bleemie's first day at her new job.

"What's your first name?"

"You have nice hair."

"He just cursed me in Persian."

"Are you married?"

The "Russian Connection," New York

"Do you give a lot of homework?"

"Boys. Boys! Boys!"

No response. Bleemie slammed down a book. Not one boy noticed. She turned the lights off. Nothing changed. She walked up to the biggest boy she saw, looked him square in the eye and said clearly and demandingly, "SIT DOWN NOW!" He sat down and looked up sheepishly. Bleemie turned her gaze around the classroom, glaring ferociously at each boy until they in turn simmered down and sat down.

"No talking without raising hands. Is that clear? Until I call on you, you are quiet."

"Boy, she's a mean witch," one boy whispered in Russian.

"You," to the whisperer. "Do you have something to say?" A long meaningful stare.

"No. Nothing." he stammered.

"Open your *Chumashim*. I am writing the *passuk* on the board."

There was rustling as the boys took out their supplies, but there was blessed silence. Bleemie began her lesson in the way she always taught *Chumash*. She was no believer in new-fangled methods of *chinuch*. What worked in *chedarim* of old she considered to be part of *Mesorah*.

"*Vayomer Hashem,* and Hashem said; *El Avram,* to Avram; *Lech Lecha,* go for your own sake ..." The whole class chanted together.

"Man, this is childish garbage," burst out the tall boy in the back of the classroom.

"Yeah, our old teacher never made us do this."

"Um, excuse me, mister," she drawled, her voice dripping with condescension, "gaining knowledge is never childish. Translate the *passuk* for me."

"*Va — Vayo — yo — mer.*" He stumbled over the pronunciation.

"Not knowing is what is childish garbage. By the time you leave my class you will not only know how to read your *Chumash* fluently without mumbling, but you will also know what it means. Is that clear?"

"Man, this is ?&*^%$."

"I beg your pardon?"

Dead silence reigned over the classroom. Bleemie walked up to the boy and looked him up and down.

"If ever I hear a word like that again, you will go to the nearest sink and wash your mouth out with soap and water."

She turned to face the rest of the class, allowing her eyes to fall on each one separately, so each boy should feel the weight of her words. "All of you. I will not allow a yeshiva boy to speak like a street boy. Such language will never be used by you."

During recess, as Bleemie supervised the boys in the yard, she heard snatches of their complaints to kids from other grades.

"She's a witch, man."

"Pow, I wish I could just blow her away."

"She said she would wash out our mouths with soap."

"She makes us chant like babies."

She also had time to study them at great length. There was a short "lil' prof," who wandered about the schoolyard humming to himself and picking up bottle caps, string and other valuable garbage. There was a tall, green-eyed bully and a stocky kid who kept trying to make conversation with her. There were two cousins, both dark, lithe and sparkling with life. In all, there were 23 little souls entrusted to her care. Bleemie surveyed her students again.

"What have I gotten myself into now?" she thought ruefully.

The first lesson she learned as a teacher was that boys did not merely play. They played, fought, fought, played and then fought some more. They climbed roofs, gates and trees, turned over furniture, collected garbage and loved tackle football. Bleemie did not give any indication that she understood every word being said in Russian. She was saving that information for a time of dire need.

Bleemie would have been content to sit on the sidelines during recess and store information for use in the classroom, but the constant fist-fighting did not allow her that luxury. It seemed that every five minutes she would have to step between flying feet and fists, ducking blows, to stop a seeming struggle-to-the-death battle.

What prompted the boys to try to kill each other? After a few sessions, she decided that most of it arose from competition in sports and devised a solution. She joined the games.

When the rivalry became too fierce, Bleemie would mess up the game by pulling a stunt that left her students wondering as to her sanity. When tensions would escalate in the midst of a soccer game, Bleemie would grab the ball, run a few yards to a line and scream, "Touchdown!"

"*Morah*, that's football," some would try to explain. The other students would just throw up their hands in disgust.

"Man, girls don't know *anything*!" They would all shake their heads in dismay at her seeming inability to comprehend sports; but fist-fighting during recess was definitely on the wane.

Chapter Twenty-One

∞ For Whom Do You Teach?

Tanya and Miriam compared letters from Bleemie. In both she described what teaching in America was like.

"They CAN keep Shabbos, but don't," Bleemie had written in big block letters with bold underlining.

Tanya wrote back promptly, "Tell your students we feel sorry for them that it is hard for them to keep Shabbos because of the many distractions."

Bleemie had smiled as she read the letter. It just increased her frustration at her inability to reach her students here in America. Although the majority of her Kiev students continued to be a source of *nachas* for her, her New York students were a nightmare. True, some did take on some *mitzvos* and seemed a bit interested, but overall the class seemed more interested in Mike Tyson than in Moshe *Rabeinu*.

After a particularly trying week, Bleemie walked into the principal's office and wearily dumped her books on his desk.

"I give up, Rabbi Berlin," she announced. "It's just too frustrating working here. In Russia, within three months, I had students who were totally observant. These kids you want me to teach are just regular smutty public school kids who don't give a hoot about *Yiddishkeit*."

"What happened now?"

"A kid brought a pornographic magazine to my class."

Rabbi Berlin nodded his head sypathetically. "Genya told me about it. I'm dealing with it right now. You're not quitting, Miss Kleiner. We need you here." He rose from his seat and headed towards the door. With his hand on the knob, he turned and face the flabbergasted young woman.

"One last thing, Miss Kleiner. I think you should go speak to Mr. Israel, the Chairman of the Board. I think it would help you to hear why he is involved in the school. I'll have Genya set that up." And with that, he was gone from the office.

Bleemie stared after him, blew out a dejected breath, and gathered her books together. As she headed towards the time clock to punch out, she ran into Genya, the school secretary.

"How are you doing?" Genya asked, slinging her arm around Bleemie.

"As usual."

"Rabbi Berlin had me call Mr. Israel for you."

"Boy, he doesn't waste any time, does he?"

"No, not him. You can meet with Mr. Israel at 8 o'clock tonight." Genya looked at Bleemie curiously. "What is this all about?"

"About the fact that I hate teaching here."

Genya looked insulted.

"I don't really hate it," Bleemie quickly corrected herself. "I'm just frustrated that I'm not getting through to these boys."

"I think you are," said Genya. Bleemie just shrugged.

Later that night, Bleemie went over to the Israel home. She had expected an opulent brick home, yet while the Israel home was brick, it was small and warm. Mr. and Mrs. Israel were the most down-to-earth people she could have hoped to find. The house was immaculate and smelled of baking cookies. Mrs. Israel had half-moon glasses, wrinkles and the nicest smile. Mr. Israel had bifocals, a potbelly and the heartiest laugh that Bleemie had ever heard. Over tea and cookies, Bleemie managed to articulate her dreams for her students, her frustrations, and what she deemed her failures. The two listened intently, Mrs. Israel occasionally reaching out to pat Bleemie's hand.

"I've noticed you quoted Reb Yaakov," said Mr. Israel, after listening quietly for some time. "There's something else he said that you should be aware of."

"Hm?"

"He said if we are at least able to help this first generation of Russian Jews remain with a strong Jewish identity, their children will have a chance to be *frum*."

"How am I helping them with their Jewish identity? Their heroes are the scum-of-the-earth rappers, their favorite pastime is watching violent shows like Power Rangers. The only reason they come to a Jewish school is because their parents are smart enough not to want their kids in public school."

"That's also a *madreigah*." Mr. Israel said softly.

Bleemie nodded her head. "One of my kids from Kiev ended up in public school here. Her parents were too closeminded to hear a word I said about the drug abuse, the lack of any morals whatsoever. You want to know what she looks like today? A drugged-out, dread-locked Jewish girl with a Puerto Rican boyfriend! So these parents are smarter than that."

"Yes, and because of that, their children stand a chance."

"They don't, Mr. Israel, they don't."

"Why don't they?"

"Because at that *Melaveh Malkah* I worked so hard to organize for the school, only 10 parents showed up. Most of the others are horrible. They don't even really care about their children."

"That's not fair."

"Oh, no? Well, you should see what I see, then. I have students whose parents are never home. The kid comes home to an empty apartment, makes himself supper, puts himself to sleep —"

Mr. Israel cut her off sharply. "What's wrong with you?" he asked angrily. "Are you going to support the family? Do you think the parents like working two jobs? They're driven to succeed, to make money to enable their children to live the American dream."

"The American dream," Bleemie muttered, rolling her eyes. "The dream of destroying the family unit."

"I'm not saying the dream is a right one, Bleemie. I'm saying that you have to understand where they're coming from — the struggles they're going through. And realize they do this because they do care about their children."

Bleemie looked down at the table, ashamed at her harsh pre-judgment. "I suppose I was being unfair," she conceded quietly. "It's just too hard."

"Let me ask you this. Why do you teach, whether it's here or in Russia?"

Bleemie felt insulted by the question. Wasn't the answer obvious? Mr. Israel did not wait for her reply, but continued. "Hopefully you do so because that is what Hashem wants you to do. You have to teach, but not because you want success. Hopefully you'll have it. But lack of success does not mean Hashem absolves you from the job of teaching."

Mr. Israel paused, and took a sip of his cooling tea. He looked directly at Bleemie, who seemed to be intently studying the pattern of the lace tablecloth.

"Do you think your students in Kiev are *frum* because of you?"

Bleemie looked up, startled.

"No," continued Mr. Israel emphatically. "You taught. That was your job. They became *frum*. That was their job. One does not have anything to do with the other. Your job is to teach. Whether or not these kids become religious is irrelevant. Aish HaTorah has this new student. She had gone to Bais Yaakov when she first came from Russia, then dropped out. Probably the teachers thought they wasted their time. Now, 15 years later, she's come back to *Yiddishkeit*."

Mr. Israel smiled warmly at the chastened young woman. "Put in your time. Don't do it for results. Do it because that is what Hashem wants us to do."

It was a humbled Bleemie who walked out of the Israel home an hour later. She realized how much of her pride had been involved in her teaching, and how wrong she had been. Thinking back to the petty fights she had had with her co-teachers in Kiev, she realized with dismay that she was a bossy know-it-all, who seemed to be doing the right things, but had the wrong motives.

"What Hashem wants you to do, you have to do," she kept re-peating in her mind. There can't be any "I" involved, any glorification sought, no success stories to boast of — just doing the work that Hashem demands of us.

"What Hashem wants you to do , you have to do!"
Baking matzohs with fifth-grade Russian boys.

She remembered something that her father had told her, something she had thought was just a "nice" story that he was sharing. Now she realized that her father had wanted her to analyze her motives.

"You think you have *ahavas Yisrael?*" her father had asked when she showed off some of her Kiev students. He told her a story.

> *There was a man in Debrecen named Rosenfeld. Reb Rosenfeld would go to the hospital and visit the Jewish patients to see what he could do for them. One day, on his rounds, he encountered an assimilated old Jew, bitter against life, bitter against Judaism, bitter against the whole world.*
>
> *Reb Rosenfeld walked into this man's hospital room, and with a warm smile gave the man what was in those days a rare item, a citrus fruit. The man looked up distrustfully.*
>
> *"Why are you giving this to me?" he demanded.*
>
> *Reb Rosenfeld said simply, "Because you are a Jew."*
>
> *"No, I'm not any more. I even wrote a will requesting crema-tion, so you shouldn't give this to me," and so saying, the man thrust the fruit back at Reb Rosenfeld.*

> *Reb Rosenfeld smiled kindly at the old man, returned the fruit to him, and said, "You are still a Jew. Here, I want you to have this, no matter what your beliefs are, no matter what plans you have made."*
>
> *The man took the fruit, insisting, "But I'll still be cremated. Just you wait and see."*
>
> *A few days passed and Reb Rosenfeld visited with the man every day, making conversation, cheering him up. And every day, the man would end off, "I'm still no Jew. I'm still going to be cremated."*
>
> *Then one day, the walls around this old man's heart finally broke down. Reb Rosenfeld and the man discussed Hashem and death. When the man died later in the week, he died saying Shema, having changed his will to state he wished to be buried k'das u'k'din.*

Mr. Kleiner had ended his story and mused for a while. Then he had said to Bleemie, "You think you have *ahavas Yisrael* because you're reaching out to these people. Ah, that's easy. You'll see results. You'll see them get married, have children. That's no trick, to want to teach them. Reb Rosenfeld had true *ahavas Yisrael*. The man was going to die in a few days, no *nachas* was expected, and yet Reb Rosenfeld cared. That is true *ahavas Yisrael*."

Now, thinking back to her father's words, Bleemie realized she had a long way to go to learn how to love Hashem, to truly love a fellow Jew, and how to go about the task Hashem sets for us.

The next week, Bleemie received a call from Mrs. Israel.

"I want to tell you something that just happened," said the bubbly *Bubbe*, as Bleemie thought of her. "We had Menachem over for Shabbos." Menachem was Bleemie's prize student.

"Didn't you have *nachas*?" asked Bleemie.

"My friends and I were amazed by him. Anyway, my husband asked him how many children in the school are like him. He said about one out of five. My husband was visibly upset. He encourages the teachers, but sometimes it *is* frustrating to see such small numbers."

"I know the feeling," said Bleemie.

"Wait, you have to hear what Menachem said. He said, 'But, Mr. Israel, didn't only 20 percent of the Jews leave Mitzrayim? It's the same numbers! Moshe did not give up his work because of the four out of five who did not want to leave Mitzrayim. He focused on the one out of five.' "

"Wow!" Bleemie was silent for a moment, thinking it over. "Thanks so much for calling. It gives me new strength to go on. *Kiruv* here in America is so much harder than in Russia, but I'm beginning to see why. In America the Jewish community is too steeped in secular culture, trying to blend in."

"Exactly," conceded Mrs. Israel. "I'm glad I called. I was worried about you. You looked so upset that night. Now you sound much better."

"Um, Mrs. Israel —"

"Yes?"

"Tell your husband I send my thanks — I think he saw right through me to my silly pride. Ever since that conversation, teaching has been a whole new experience for me."

Bleemie paused for a moment. "And can you please tell him that for a change I'm teaching for Hashem and not for my own glorification."

Four wonderful reasons for "teaching for Hashem and not for my own glorification."
The first boy on the right is Shloma Sofer — a direct descendant of the Chasam Sofer. He now lives in Brooklyn.

Chapter Twenty-Two

∞ To Give Is to Get

Mrs. Kleiner, former principal of Bais Yaakov, was a fount of teaching advice. Bleemie's most successful teaching projects were her mother's.

"Mommy, how do I get them to remember to wear their *tzitzis*?" asked Bleemie one day.

"Make it a school-wide effort. Walk the halls and randomly ask boys if they are wearing them. If they are, give them a candy."

Bleemie became the candy teacher, not just for her students, but for any student she encountered. Almost every boy in the school began wearing *tzitzis* in quest of the candy. One little boy came over to Bleemie in the hall. He looked up at her with sparkling eyes. "Um, excuse me, *Morah*," he said, his pudgy finger pointing to her.

"Yes?"

"*Morah*, look, I'm wearing seven *tzitzis*. Now give me my seven candies."

"But you only are supposed to wear one pair." Bleemie could not help smiling.

The boy kept his hand out for his candy. "Reuven told me that if one pair of *tzitzis* gets one candy," and he stabbed his finger into his palm emphatically, "seven pairs get seven candies."

It figured that Reuven had something to do with it. Reuven was Bleemie's "problem" student, always out to do mischief. His antics always brought laughter, but Bleemie did not know how to reach him in terms of teaching. He was not absorbing most of what she taught, and the little that got through, he used for pranks.

During lunchtime, Bleemie circulated through the dining room making sure everybody made the proper *brachos*. By now she was able to spot the newcomers. One day she called over a new boy. "Come here and make a *brachah*. I'll teach you what to say."

"It's all right," the boy reassured her with an airy wave of his hand. "Reuven already taught me."

Bleemie's eyebrow lifted in surprise. Reuven? She shrugged to herself, then said to the boy, "Okay. Wash."

The boy washed carefully, properly. Bleemie was impressed.

The boy turned, lifted his hands, and, with a swoosh, sprinkled every last drop of water on the boys standing in back of him. Bleemie smiled. That would be Reuven's style.

"Now make the *brachah*," instructed Bleemie.

Russian boys learning about davening and tzitzis in Brooklyn.

"Baruch Ata Ado-nai ..." Reuven had done a great job of teaching, *"... shelo asani melech."*

"What?" Hmmm! So much for Reuven's helpful streak.

That night, Mrs. Kleiner was consulted. "What am I going to do with that Reuven, Mommy?"

"I have an idea," said Mrs. Kleiner. "You told me he likes music?"

"Yup, he, and just about every other boy in America, wants to be a rock star."

"Let me make a call and see what happens."

Bleemie was wondering whom her mother would call, but since the information wasn't volunteered she didn't ask. Two days later, her mother brought up the subject.

"You know cousin Shimon has been out of things since the accident —"

Bleemie nodded. That whole accident story had been something out of a horror movie.

Shimon had been backing out of the family driveway when his younger brother darted behind the car. The child survived, but with multiple handicaps. Both internally and externally, he had literally been crushed by the car.

As much as people told Shimon that it had not been his fault, he had withdrawn into himself in misery. The once outgoing, charismatic young man had become a silent, haunted specter of himself.

"I called him," said Mrs. Kleiner, "and convinced him to volunteer twice a week with Reuven."

"Mommy, that's great!" exclaimed Bleemie. "Why didn't I think of that — Shimon the guitar whiz — of course! That's just what Reuven needs. They can sit all day strumming and being groovy."

Shimon began teaching the Russian boy how to play guitar, as well as how to apply himself to his studies. Within a month, Bleemie noticed a difference in Reuven's behavior. He was still brimming with mischief, his green eyes still danced with naughty ideas, but more and more he began resembling a yeshiva boy.

"Gosh, it worked, Mommy," Bleemie commented in awe. "Reuven is becoming a whole different person. I haven't heard him curse in about a week."

"It worked for Shimon, too," said her mother quietly.

Bleemie did not understand her mother's words until a week later, when her cousin came to visit.

Bleemie was shocked at his appearance. Shimon had once been considered the best-looking Kleiner grandchild, known for his pleasant face, great grin and brilliant blue eyes. Since the accident, two lines had appeared about his mouth, and his eyes looked almost vacant. He looked years older than his age. Bleemie shuddered and turned her eyes away.

"So, do you want to discuss the student you foisted on me?"

Bleemie realized Shimon was speaking to her and quickly looked back up.

"He's really doing well, Shimon. I can't tell you how great this has been for him." Bleemie felt odd speaking to Shimon, as if since the accident he had become a different person than the cousin she'd grown up with. Her voice was stiff and formal, her words tripping over themselves in her haste to end the conversation. Shimon nodded, then dropped into a swivel chair. "Do you have any other kids you want me to work with?"

Bleemie's eyes widened in surprise. "Sure. You can start working with another one of my bullies any time you want to."

Shimon swiveled around a few times. "Did you hear that Reuven called me — collect, mind you — at midnight — to let me know his father promised him a guitar for his birthday?" Shimon laughed.

Bleemie stared. The two lines were still furrowed in his cheek, but when he laughed, a little bit of the old Shimon emerged and his eyes came back to life.

Mrs. Kleiner came to the table with a plate of cake. "Stop swiveling and make a *brachah*," she instructed her nephew.

Bleemie noted her mother spoke to Shimon as warmly as she always had, in a teasing, affectionate tone "Gosh," thought Bleemie with a guilty start, "maybe I should start pretending nothing's changed since the accident. Maybe that's what Shimon wants people to start doing."

"One more swivel," Shimon said with a half-grin. He picked up a piece of cake. "Thanks, *Tante*."

"Sir, since when do you need to thank me for stopping your swiveling?"

Shimon became serious. "Not that. You know —" He was looking down at the cake, absentmindedly crumbling it. "You hooked me up with Reuven — I suppose I couldn't go on —"

Mrs. Kleiner nodded.

"I'm beginning to realize there is still a lot Hashem wants for me to do in life. What happened — you know — the whole thing —"

Shimon closed his eyes and took a deep breath. "Now I see it's a stumbling block of the *Yetzer Hara*. I almost gave up on life. What I didn't realize is that the only way to get back at the *Yetzer Hara* is by doing the opposite. With every good thing I do, I'm making a statement that I won't be beaten. Every time I'm able to accomplish something, I'm hitting back at him, big time."

Bleemie listened in amazement. "I don't think I would be able to survive if something like that had happened to me," she confided to her mother after Shimon had left.

"You have to realize something that Shimon has begun to realize, Bleemie. Many times, tragedy is a tool of the *Satan*. He tries to break our spirit. If we get caught up in our sorrow, we let him win. If we strike back by doing good things, like tutoring Reuven, we're dealing the *Satan* another blow."

"I don't know, Mommy. Sounds good in theory, but I can't imagine going on in life after something so horrid."

"Life goes on regardless of our feelings. It's what we do with it that shows who we really are. If you look outside of your own emotional state, and push yourself to give to others, then the ongoing life has value and meaning."

"I suppose you can then say to give is to get," said Bleemie slowly.

"Absolutely," replied her mother. "Look at Shimon. He received more than Reuven. He found a reason to come out of his personal sorrow. And don't forget to look at yourself.

"Yes, ma'am. At you. Face it, Bleemie. When you started on this whole Russian outreach part of your life, you weren't — how should I say this — exactly a polished, mature, sensitive person."

"Child horror, that was me," said Bleemie in a droll tone, pulling a monster face.

"Pretty close to that," teased Mrs. Kleiner. Then, in a more serious vein, "No, you weren't a child horror, not by any stretch of the imagination. But you weren't a rounded-out grownup either, until you started taking on responsibility. Since you've understood other people's needs and pains, you've become a more sensitive person."

"Can you really see that I'm changing, Mommy?" asked Bleemie.

"You're a whole different person, Bleemie. Don't get me wrong. We always loved you at every stage of your growth. But until we start accomplishing things, the greatness inside of us is mere potential, like unmined diamonds. Every time we do something, we're unearthing the diamonds and making them appear."

"To give is to get," said Bleemie again. "I actually do feel myself changing every day. Maybe — just maybe — if I keep this up, someday, I just might make you proud."

"*Shayfela*, we've always been proud," said her mother.

"Yeah, but maybe someday, I'll grow up to the point where I won't make you and Tatty cringe with my devil-may-care attitude. And maybe I'll learn how to keep my big mouth shut where appropriate."

"That would be nice," agreed Mrs. Kleiner with a smile. "And for starters, do you think you can give up the notion that every time you speak to a *shadchan*, you have to say something to shock her?"

Bleemie laughed. "So Mrs. Stern did not think it normal for a girl to say she wants someone to come riding along in a white Porsche?" Bleemie giggled as she thought of the dismay on the *shadchan's* face at that comment, then grew serious again. "I'll try, Mommy, I really will."

Bleemie mulled over that discussion for days. Her students and their parents had often sent little gifts and thank-you letters to her. She began to realize it was she who should be thanking them. "*Mikal milamdai hiskalti.*" She now realized just how much she had learned, both in Kiev, and now in America.

Chapter Twenty-Three

∞ The Visitor

Tanya sat side by side with Miriam, holding her hand. After all the letter writing back and forth between Bleemie and Tanya, the dream that the Russian girl had feared would never become reality was being fulfilled.

It was frightening to be on a plane for the first time. The takeoff of the plane had made her stomach drop and lurch. Her heart had been doing that drop-and-lurch routine ever since she had boarded. It had nothing to do with the movement of the plane, and everything to do with her realization that her movement to a life committed to Torah was finally in motion.

The public-address system switched on. "Attention passengers, we will be landing in Kennedy airport in 20 minutes..."

Tanya felt Miriam's hand tremble and she squeezed it, partially to reassure her friend, but mostly to relieve her own anxiety.

Tanya went through all the routines of customs like a robot, feeling as if she were in a fairy tale. She walked with her bags towards the exit. The doors swung open and she stepped out into a big hall.

∞∞

Bleemie had been making polite conversation with Tanya's relatives for the past hour as they waited for the delayed plane. These relatives were not religious, and Bleemie could tell they had high hopes that in the few days Tanya would spend with them they would be able to get a word in that would convince her to go to college.

Bleemie's eyes kept straying to the computer screen that listed the arrivals and departures. Finally she saw it: Air Ukraine: arrived.

She rushed to stand at the arrival area. The doors swung open. She didn't notice the crush of arrivals, was oblivious of those around her. All she noticed were "her" two girls. She ran headlong towards them, crying. Then she was embracing them, lifting Miriam into the air and hugging her tightly.

Tanya saw Bleemie rushing towards her, her relatives in the background. She hugged and kissed Bleemie, then moved on to greet them. She was slightly jealous that Miriam was getting the extended time with Bleemie.

Tanya was grateful to her relatives for all their material support. However, Bleemie had given her something far more precious — a meaningful goal in life, and a chance to recapture what her father never had. This woman standing here smiling at her was her dead father's sister, and she wanted to renew her relationship with her. But the girl standing there, her former teacher, was her father's champion, pushing Tanya into a life that would bring him credit in the World to Come.

The next few days were torture for Tanya. She had not realized that her relatives were so antireligious. Had she known, she would have never agreed to visit with them for such an extended period. She ate only fruits and vegetables the first day of her stay as her relatives refused to buy her anything kosher, or even take her to a kosher store. In desperation, she had called Bleemie. Bleemie had some friends deliver meals and that is how Tanya subsisted.

Tanya and her relatives said strained good-byes when her visit was over. They had failed to budge her from any of her convictions. Politely, they invited her back, knowing full well that their behavior had probably ensured she would not come again for an extended stay. With some last hugs and kisses, they said goodbye and put Tanya on a Monsey Trails bus, off to her host family.

Although the bus ride was long, and Tanya was emotionally exhausted from the difficulties of the last two weeks, anxiety kept her awake. Would her host family like her? Would she like them? How could she live with some strange family?

The bus driver turned towards her. "This is it — your stop."

Tanya gathered her bags, trying to calm herself. As she stepped off the bus, she saw a family lined up near a station wagon, waving "Welcome, Tanya" signs. The first thing she noticed was that every one of the six children had her coloring, blond hair with dark brown eyes. The next thing she noticed was the earnest eyes of the 5-year-old. He looked up and studied her from every angle. Then he told her with a serious expression, comical on one so young, "I told my father you could have my bed, but my father bought a bed just for you. Really, you could have had mine."

The relief of knowing she was wanted was too much for Tanya, and the tears began to course down her cheeks. She smiled through them in an attempt to show that they were happy tears, not sad ones. But all tears are sad for children. In two seconds, there was a flurry of small plump arms holding Tanya, and two wet kisses, compliments of Miri and Shaindy. Tanya gratefully realized that with this family she had found more than a place to stay; she had found a home.

The Steinbergs had been told of Tanya's visit with her relatives. They realized that the 16-year-old had been through an emotional wringer and kept questions to a minimum that first night. There was a hearty supper, a tour of the house, and a warm hug and goodnight kiss from Mrs. Steinberg. Then, the door to Tanya's room was firmly shut and the children were told not to bother the new guest.

The next day, Mrs. Steinberg allowed Tanya to stay home. She figured that a day of adjustment would be wise before Tanya began school. Bleemie came to visit, to show that she was available if needed.

The Steinberg children were thrilled with Tanya. "Getting a big sister is even more exciting than getting a new baby," said Shaindy. After all, babies did not let you sit on their lap.

For her second Shabbos at the Steinbergs, Tanya invited Miriam to stay with them. It had been Mrs. Steinberg's idea, one that Tanya could only respond to with a happy intake of breath and the desire to squeal with delight the way Shaindy sometimes did. Instead, she had shyly said, "Thank you so much — please, please, let me do a lot to help you with the cooking and cleaning. Please." Mrs. Steinberg had laughed and sent her off to do homework.

Friday came and Tanya could not sit still. Miriam was coming to visit! Mrs. Steinberg had wisely assigned Tanya all the tasks relating to Miriam's visit. It made Tanya feel more at home, more a part of the family.

Miriam's Shabbos visit went off without a hitch. The two girls spent hours comparing families and funny anecdotes about life in America.

For Mrs. Steinberg, the visit had been one of the most helpful tools in reaching out to Tanya, as the girl now felt comfortable around the house and family. Her timid, shy exterior fell away, and she would bubble on and on about everything to Mrs. Steinberg.

"You know my children are all small," said Mrs. Steinberg to Bleemie, "but now I know what joy it is to have a teenage daughter."

"Mommy, that lady is an angel," Bleemie reported. "Do you know that she writes letters to Tanya's mother and grandmother, thanking them for letting Tanya live with her, updating them on every little bit of news in Tanya's life? People like that are one in a million!"

Chapter Twenty-Four

∞ Listen Up, Brighton

"Grrr. I'm so angry!" said Bleemie, barging into the house one day.

Her mother looked up from the pastry dough she was rolling out. "What happened?"

"I got off the train near school and there was a Christian woman standing on the street giving out missionary stuff. She was pretty, put together, nice suit, striking up conversations with all the Russians. One *babushka* she started up with told her she didn't speak English, so the woman switched to a perfect, flawless Russian. I could have fainted!"

"The missionaries are active?"

"Active? They crawl all over the Brighton Beach neighborhood like cockroaches. They even offered money to one of my student's parents to convince them to switch him to a Catholic school. Baruch Hashem, we found out about it, but Rabbi Berlin had a hard time convincing the parents not to send him."

"What can be done about it?"

"Heaven only knows. I don't. It really stumps me. How do I answer a parent who called to ask why we killed Yushke?"

"Is there any organization that is doing something about the missionaries?" asked Mrs. Kleiner.

"There is some stuff COJO does, the JCRC, here and there various small things. But even in Kiev we had the same problem. These missionaries have huge budgets to work with. They give out free literature, have these great concerts and offer money. We have nothing like that."

"Maybe we should," said Mrs. Kleiner.

"Um, are you volunteering our family for some more work, Mommy?" asked Laya.

Bleemie laughed at the expression on her sister's face. Bleemie favorite saying was, "Family is great. Family can't say no, while others can." And she used that to the fullest extent. This time, though, it was her mother who was doing the recruiting.

"Actually, I think all Bleemie's students should get involved. Let the girls from Kiev also do something. People did for them — now they should do for others."

"What do you have in mind?"

"I don't know that we can do very much, but we should be able to pull off a concert," said Mrs. Kleiner, not realizing that her comment would come under the category of "Famous Last Words"!

"I never realized my idea would be this much work," Mrs. Kleiner confided to her husband.

"Yet once you start something, you won't back off until you've accomplished your goal," replied her husband with a grin. "Guess we know where Bleemie gets her genes."

"Did you know that we need to get a permit to have the concert?"

"I'll tell you what — let me discuss it with some people I know. Maybe I can get some help."

True to his word, Mr. Kleiner spoke to business colleagues and *shul* friends. Thanks to him, the concert became more and more of a reality. One person managed to push the applications through the right channels, and a permit was given to have the concert on the beach. Another one found sponsorship for food. Yet another got three famous singers to agree to perform.

Bleemie recruited her former students and the staff at Yeshiva Academy. Each day brought new ideas tumbling forth.

"We'll call every organization that does Russian outreach and have them set up information tables at the concert," said Rabbi Berlin one day. The principal had thrown himself into the thick of the work of organizing the concert.

Another organization, *Shamir,* promised to donate a book to every attendee.

"I'm doing a clothing drive and we'll have clothing racks where people can take outfits if they want," said Laya.

Bleemie's students circulated flyers, made phone calls to Russian couples, and got set to be hostesses at the concert. "Lighten Up Brighton" was off and flying. Regina had done beautiful artwork for the flyers and posters. The girls had spent hours walking around Brighton Beach, taping notices on every available pole.

"You know what is most frustrating, Mommy," said Bleemie right before the concert. "Now, that we've done all the hard work, every-one wants to be listed as a sponsor."

"Bleemie, that's the way the world has always been. Who cares? The important thing is that people should get involved."

At the concert, Bleemie looked around with pride. Her students comprised most of the staff. Tanya, newly arrived from Kiev, had been appointed security person. She was standing at the bottom of the stage steps, surrounded by the children of the family with whom she lived. "Isn't it funny?" noted Bleemie to her mother as they passed by carrying refreshments for the performers, "Tanya looks so much like the Steinberg family, right down to her coloring."

Mrs. Kleiner looked at Tanya and the children and nodded. "She looks as if she's adjusting to America really well."

"The adjustment is hard, but the Steinbergs are wonderful to her. They treat her like a part of the family. Look." The two smiled as they watched Tanya with her arms around Miri and Shaindy.

"Show me how to use the walkie-talkie," begged Miri of Tanya.

"You press zis button and talk."

"What are we supposed to be doing?" asked Shaindy.

"We make sure nobody goes up zere," explained Tanya, pointing to the stage steps, "unless zey are supposed to." She showed the children the program and pointed to the barrier. "See zis rope. We don't open it for anyone who is not on zis list."

Shaindy nodded seriously. "Okay, Miri," she said, "you stand on that side of the rope, I'll stand here, and Tanya will stand in middle. That way we won't let anyone onto stage." The two little girls took up their positions, their faces solemn with responsibility.

Just then, a politician approached with his entourage. He started towards the steps.

"Excuse me," said Tanya in her thick accent, "you can't go zere."

The two little girls came close to Tanya. "Tanya is the guard," piped up Shaindy, "and we're helping her."

The man did not deign to reply. He let one of his aides do the talking, as he busied himself with earnest conversation with another aide. "This is a very important gentleman," explained the spokesman to Tanya. "He put together this event and is supposed to be speaking. And you really shouldn't have little childen back here."

"We're not little," Miri said indignantly, "and we're helping Tanya."

Tanya blushed in confusion. She did not remember any such speaker as part of the program. "Um, wait just a moment please," she said, as she picked up her walkie-talkie.

"Let me, let me," clamored Miri.

"Here, you press ze button and I will talk," instructed Tanya, crouching down beside Miri.

"This is beyond ridiculous," burst out the aide.

Tanya ignored him. Miri pressed the button, and Tanya spoke, "Mr. Kleiner?" The radio crackled back, "Yes, Tanya?" "Mr. Kleiner, there's a man here who wants to go on ze stage —"

By this time, the important gentleman and his aides were tapping their feet impatiently. Tanya was parked in front of them, her hand firmly on the rope stanchion, not budging. Short of stepping over her and the children or shoving them out of the way, there was no way they were able to get onto the stage. "Will you open that rope already!"

At that point, Mr. Kleiner, Rabbi Berlin and some of the other actual organizers came up behind them. Tanya thankfully moved to a side, allowing the men to take over.

"Excuse me," said Rabbi Berlin, "is there a problem?"

The aide turned around. "Yes," he said rudely, "there is a problem. My boss is supposed to be speaking and he needs to get on stage.

"Correction," said Rabbi Berlin pleasantly. "Your employer is not supposed to be speaking. This is not a political rally. I invited the community to show the Brighton Beach people that it cares, not to collect votes."

The would-be speaker's face reddened a bit, but, being a true public servant, he smiled and said, "Of course. It's really nice to meet you, Rabbi Berlin. Good work that you're doing."

One aide had to get in a parting shot, "You really shouldn't have children here," he said pointing to the young Steinbergs.

"They seem to be doing a very fine job," said Mr. Kleiner with a smile.

Mr. Kleiner turned to Tanya, "You're doing great. Now back on the job, all three of you." Miri and Shaindy bounced back to the rope stanchion.

"Right we are good guards?" asked Shaindy.

"The best," replied Mr. Kleiner. "Do you want me to bring you all some donuts?"

"Donuts, yum?"

Tanya walked back to the rope, a little shaky from the confrontation. For the millionth time that day, she felt thankful for the fact that she had Shaindy and Miri here to boost her self-confidence.

A performer arrived and Tanya opened the stanchion to allow him to pass. As he headed up the steps, Shaindy pointed to Tanya and called after the performer, "She's my sister."

"Really?" said the performer politely, not bothering to turn around.

"A new sister," shouted Shaindy, as the man disappeared onto stage.

"Sh!" giggled Tanya, gathering up Shaindy in a thankful hug.

The concert was a huge success. Although the press quoted several people who had been there as being "deeply concerned" about the problem of missionaries snatching Jewish souls, Bleemie knew that most of the hard work of organizing and running the concert had been done by her former students.

"Giving back," was the way Mrs. Kleiner termed it. "Passing along what they got," was Mr. Kleiner's view.

"Okay, tonight is party time!" Bleemie announced to the girls. "My mother promised you all a slumber party if we pulled this concert off, remember? Let's go!"

"I don't know which is more fun, the concert or the party," said Tanya later that night, after the third round of popcorn and potato chips.

"I don't know which was more fun," responded Bleemie with a yawn. "The fun is about to end, because I am zonked. Into nightgowns, folks. Bedtime!"

The girls began scrambling about, pulling nightgowns from shopping bags, hefting pillows at one another, and forming a line for the bathroom.

Miriam went in first. "Uh oh," she called out, "I think I broke your toilet. It doesn't flush."

"No, you didn't break it," Bleemie called back. "Sometimes the chain falls off." That chain was a legendary nuisance in the Kleiner house. Every now and then it would fall off and the flushing mechanism would not work.

"The chain?" asked Miriam.

"You know how a toilet works?"

"N-o-o."

"Pick up the top of the tank," instructed Bleemie. She heard the rattle of cosmetics from the top of the tank. "Now pull the chain."

"There's no chain," Miriam wailed.

"Just pull up the black thing," called Bleemie.

There was a moment of silence, then a piercing shriek from the bathroom, followed by the sound of rushing water. Sure enough, Miriam had pulled the wrong "black thing" and the toilet tank erupted into a minigeyser.

"Bleemie, get in here quick," screamed Miriam.

So much for going to sleep! It took two hours to mop up and sop up the gallons of water that had seeped into the living room.

"This never happened in Russia," said Miriam, after the mess had been cleared.

"Right," said Bleemie, "because you don't have toilets in Russia."

"That's not true," the girls protested, almost as if one.

"Okay, so you have some real old ones in some of the fancier apartments."

"Bleemie, why are you always trying to make Russia seem more backwards than it is?" demanded Tanya angrily. "I hear you tell people how backwards Russia is and how people starve. That's not true."

Bleemie blinked in surprise. She knew the facts as she stated them were true. After all, she had seen life in Russia first hand. In what other so-called modern country would one find old *babushkas* painting the lines in the street by hand, or see rows and rows of windows with food hanging out of them to keep cold, because there were no refrigerators? How horrified she had been to see a nurse vaccinate an entire school with the same unsterilized needle!

"But it is true, Tanya," protested Bleemie. "Maybe not everybody is starving. But you find so many people who are."

"You make it worse than it is," insisted Tanya, with an angry toss of her head. "I mean, we do have toilets."

In response, Bleemie opened a drawer in her dresser, and pulled out an envelope of pictures. "Want to see the pictures I took in Russia?" she invited.

The girls passed around the photos, commenting on each one.

"There you are, Jana."

"Remember that Sunday at Bnot Chayil?"

"That's a great shot of our class."

"Ooh, here's one of the Purim party!"

"Bleemie," a shocked voice broke through, "why did you take a picture of this?" Jana held up a photo of the bathroom in the Hebrew School, which consisted of tiled holes in the ground — no toilets, no stalls, just a nice neat row of holes.

"Maybe it is true," muttered Tanya, her face turning beet red, "but you don't have to keep reminding us."

"You see, Bleemie," said another girl softly, "we came from that country and every time you say how bad it is, it makes us feel as if you're saying we're also backwards."

Now Bleemie understood the protests. For a long time she had wondered why she found the immigrants negating her version of what life was like in Russia. She would talk of hunger and ask for food donations, and her students would wave a dismissive hand and say, "They could use food, but nobody is starving." She could talk about the lack of medical care, and the immigrants would frown and say, "I never had a problem with my health."

Bleemie resolved to be more careful about speaking negatively about Russia in the presence of her former students. She realized now that they were sensitive to the criticism, taking it as a reflection on themselves.

"It's okay, girls," she announced, gathering up her pictures, "the country you left behind might be backwards, but you are the classiest lot of young ladies I've ever had the good fortune to meet. And definitely the best concert organizers!"

Chapter Twenty-Five

∞ To Pay the Piper

Bleemie arrived at work one day to find many gloomy faces in the teachers' room. That wasn't so unusual anymore, as Yeshiva Academy had not been able to meet its payroll for many weeks.

Today, things were coming to a head. "If we walk out, will you walk out with us?" asked Mrs. Katz of Bleemie. Bleemie had heard the teachers discussing that option, threatening the administration with it, even writing up a formal protest to the board members. Yet, she never thought it would actually happen. Who were they walking out on? The administration? No, it would be the students who would lose out.

"I don't think so," said Bleemie carefully. She knew that all the teachers were waiting to hear her response. "I can't walk out on my students."

There was a babble of voices as the argument swirled around the teachers' room. If the walkout was not unanimous, would it pay for some to leave anyway?

"It's different for her," said Mrs. Katz, pointing to Bleemie. "She's single and doesn't need the money. I support my family by teaching. I can't tell my landlord to wait another few months!"

"She's right," said Bleemie to all who were listening. "For me, the money is not crucial."

Bleemie smiled grimly as she said that. Money was also crucial to her although she didn't have to worry about being evicted. She too was deeply in debt. Tanya had needed dental work, and Bleemie had made an appointment with a *frum* dentist. After examining Tanya and making copious notes of all the work that needed to be done, the dentist had looked at Bleemie and said, "I do have to get paid, you know. I'll give you a 10 percent discount, but the rest is up to you."

"Deeper and deeper into debt I go," thought Bleemie, but she was totally unprepared for the staggering amount of the bill when it finally came — $680 after the 10 percent discount! Yeshiva Academy had not given her a paycheck in three months, and Bleemie still owed money for Miriam's tuition.

"I haven't bought one new outfit this year," thought Bleemie with a guilty start. Her mother frequently told her that what she was doing was not right

"You are not allowed to give away that much money to *tzedakah.*"

Bleemie hated "*shnorring,*" however, and would rather empty her own pockets before asking anyone for a donation. Unfortunately, her pockets had been empty for some time without any hope of a monetary infusion. She knew, also, that most of the other teachers were in even worse situations. Many were *Kollel* wives, supporting their families while their husbands learned. Not receiving their paycheck literally meant not having money for rent and food.

"I suppose we should ask a Rav what to do," said Bleemie to the teachers.

"I discussed it with my Rav already," said Mrs. Katz.

"So that's what we'll do," said Bleemie decisively, relieved at not having to put anyone, herself certainly included, in the awkward position of making an unpopular decision. "Each one of us will call her own Rav. Then we'll see who should walk out and who should not."

Bleemie was told not to walk out. She wondered what the scene would be like in the teachers' room the next day and what would happen to the children whose teachers did walk out. The phone rang that evening as she was preparing her lessons.

"Bleemie? It's Mr. Israel."

"Hi, Mr. Israel."

"I need you to tell me what's going on in school."

Bleemie hesitated. She did not want to be in the position of repeating school politics to the chairman of the board.

"Look," continued Mr. Israel, "I've heard that the teachers want to walk out. I have to know if they will or won't."

"Some of them want to," Bleemie reluctantly admitted.

"Will they?"

"It looks that way. We decided today that we would ask *Daas Torah* what to do."

"Look, Bleemie, let me explain why I'm asking this. I don't want you to play informer. I don't want to get rid of those who feel that they need to walk out. They have good cause, but we have no money. Tonight I was able to get a few donations. I just want to know whom I should pay first to make sure our students have teachers."

Oh, now that he put it that way — Bleemie quickly told him which teachers were desperately in need of their paychecks.

The next day, there was quiet in the teachers' room. Mr. Israel had come down and spent an hour speaking to the teachers. Bleemie noted how tired he looked. For some of them, he had checks; for others, the reassurance that he had spoken to their landlords, who had agreed to wait for the rent owed them.

For the first time, Bleemie began to understand how much went into keeping a school like Yeshiva Academy going.

She thought back to a conversation she had accidentally overheard. A week ago, the teachers had stormed Rabbi Berlin's office, hounding him about their paychecks. Afterwards, Bleemie had been standing outside the door to his office, waiting to speak to him about something else, when she overheard him speaking to his wife. He sounded close to tears.

"They are angry at me. At me. Don't they understand that I have the same problem, only worse? I have not gotten a paycheck for twice as long as they! Why can't they realize I have a landlord too, and children, and doctor bills?"

Bleemie had fled from the office, not wanting to hear any more.

A new craze was sweeping the school. It was called Virtual Pets, but to Bleemie they were Virtual Pests. They were small video games, with distinct personalities. They demanded attention and care, much as real babies do. During class, students would suddenly gasp and dive into their schoolbags to retrieve the little things. Buttons would be pushed, attention totally diverted from the lesson, followed by either a sigh of relief or a horrified mutter, "I killed it."

It took a while for the boys to explain the point of these thinga-majigs to Bleemie. The "pet" demanded food, naps and attention. If you did not comply, the thing just gave up the ghost and would "die." Even the wrath of an irate teacher would not sway a student from diverting his attention to his pet.

It was certainly the most annoying distraction that Bleemie had ever had to contend with. She wondered what the boys did about their pets on Shabbos, but was afraid to ask, sure of the answer. She knew that anyone with this type of "pet" was being *mechallel Shabbos*.

Shortly after the threatened strike, Bleemie, determined to give the board mileage for its money, was teaching a carefully researched lesson. If these people cared enough about these boys to go out and raise funds for the school, she would make sure these boys learned to care about their lessons. One boy, interested in the *Halachah* she had just taught, was asking good questions and paying attention to her patient answers.

Suddenly, a beep sounded from his schoolbag. All questions about *Halachos* were gone from his mind and Bleemie found herself talking to the empty space above his head. The boy focused his full attention on his pet. He had almost saved it when a hand reached out and snatched it from him. He looked up in shock. Bleemie stood there, holding it above his head.

"*Morah*, please," he pleaded, "it will die."

"Will it?" said Bleemie. "Well then, let it."

"*Morah*," protested all those boys who understood the boy's dilemma by virtue of the fact that they had pets too. "*Morah*, it will take a minute. That's it. But if you don't give it to him, it will die."

Bleemie ignored the pleas and walked back to her desk with the little "pet" swinging from her thumb. She sat down and looked around.

"Boys, there's something I have to tell you."

There was a mournful silence as the boys listened intently. Bleemie realized they were not listening to hear her words, but were just straining to hear the dying beeps of the "pet."

"There's a spark in every Jewish soul," said Bleemie sadly. "That spark needs attention and food, or else it dies, just like your pets. Just a minute ago, someone's spark said it needed to have a bit of *Halachah* food. And that someone ignored the spark. So the spark had to die a bit. The spark had to die because of this," Bleemie held up the Virtual Pet. "Now this should die, because it made the spark die."

There was silence that stretched on. Then the Virtual Pet croaked its last. "Oh, *Morah*, you killed it," groaned the class.

"It's better off dead," said Bleemie.

"You know how much it costs?" demanded a student.

"You know how much you cost?" Bleemie demanded in return. "Guys, do you know how much money people like Mr. Israel have to collect so you can learn? Who paid for your desk? Your chair? Your books? Your teachers? Much more money goes into your eduation than goes into these silly games." She tossed the dead game back to its owner.

"We learn, *Morah*," protested the boy. "I know lots and lots now."

"And yet, you know about Shabbos. Tell me, did you press your pet's buttons on Shabbos?"

The room was silent. Several of the boys had the grace to blush.

"So there is a death struggle between your soul's spark and your pet's. One has to die. I'd rather see your pet die than your precious spark."

"Does that mean you'll kill our pets?"

"It means that I don't want to see any more pets in class. If I see them, I take them."

Silence again, as those boys who owned pets looked at each other in wild despair. "Have your sister take care of it," muttered one boy to another.

"Oh, just let them die," piped up another, "they're babyish any-way."

And that was the last Bleemie saw of the Virtual Pests.

Chapter Twenty-Six

∞ They Do Care

Desperate for funds, Yeshiva Academy was planning a benefit concert at Carnegie Hall. Bleemie decided that her students would benefit by helping with the event, as it was rare for them to see the fun side of the Jewish world. A few phone calls, a few discussions, and with Mr. Israel's blessings, Bleemie's students were written into the program.

The boys' excitement at being included was tempered when they heard what they would have to wear on stage.

"Bow ties? That's crazy," was one reaction.

"And suspenders!" Valdimir was horrified. "Man, what do they think we are, old geezers?"

Bleemie, assuring her students that they would be a big hit at the concert, decided to get maximum mileage out of the experience. She became a one-woman publicity committee for the event, enthusing about it nonstop to her boys, building up their excitement. She hung posters of the singers who would be performing on the walls of her classroom.

When the singers came on a tour of the school, Bleemie insisted that her students see who they were. After all, as she later explained to her mother, "Since many of their heroes are singers anyway, at least let them be *frum* Jews!"

One morning, therefore, she interrupted her lesson to demand that everyone climb on his seat and look out the window. The boys needed no second invitation. In two seconds, they had all scrambled up onto their seats.

Bleemie pointed out of the window at the singers as they got out of their car. "See that man, the one with the really long *payos*? That's Yehuda Glanz, and behind him is Avraham Fried. Look, the one getting out of the car now is Mordechai Ben David."

"Wow, I see him."

"He looks like Rabbi Berlin."

"Can he sing for us?"

"I can't wait until the concert!"

Bleemie found herself impatient for concert night too. The night of the concert came, Bleemie arrived with her sister, Laya, and her friend, Malky. The three wore their fanciest suits and jewelry, even twisting their hair up into sleek chignons.

"After all, we're going to be society ladies for the night," Bleemie had insisted.

The marbled entrance area of Carnegie Hall was packed with people waiting to get in to the performance.

"I feel like I'm lost among a bear clan," Malky complained, as the three stood there waiting among the "beminked" women. Bleemie spotted a familiar face. "Ah, that's the school secretary. Genya, I'd like you to meet my friend, and this is my sister."

Just then there was a commotion behind Bleemie.

"*Morah*," shouted Mischa. He was tugging at an older woman, pulling her toward Bleemie. "This is my grandmother, *Morah*," he said proudly. Mischa's grandmother was almost as short and chubby as her grandson, with a curly, grey *shaitel* framing her double-chinned face.

"*A gitten tag*," said the grandmother, all smiles. She grabbed Bleemie's hand and kissed it effusively, much to Bleemie's chagrin and to the amusement of those around them. The curls in her *shaitel* bobbed about, as bouncy as their wearer.

"*Oy, bubbele*," said the grandmother in a mixture of Yiddish and English, "*Ich bin frim. Ya*, I keep Shabbos, *kusher, alles*." She put her hand on her chest dramatically. "My son no keep. *Oiy, yoi, yoi, yoi*," she shook her head sorrowfully.

"*Mine einikel*, Mische, Moishele, is named after my husband. If you only make him *frim*, you'll get *Oylam Hazeh, Oylam Haba*, a great husband, anything you want. Only make Mischa *frim*. *Yuh?*"

Thankfully, at that point the ushers announced the beginning of the performance. Bleemie was able to make her way into the auditorium and escape the amused glances being sent her way.

"Wow! *Classna!* This is something!" exclaimed Malky, overwhelmed at the red carpets, chandeliers and magnificent architecture. Bleemie was busy studying the people as they filed into the performance hall. "Do you think they really care," asked Bleemie suddenly, her sweeping hand indicating the audience, "or did they come just to see and be seen, to enjoy some entertainment?"

The lights dimmed as people found their seats. Softly at first, then swelling with sound, the music began playing. Malky, watching the stage intently as the blue-and-red lights spotlighting the band blinked eerily, seemed not to have heard Bleemie's question. Bleemie nudged her friend with an elbow. "Do you think they really care?"

"Shhh!" Malky replied, "I want to listen to the music."

Bleemie turned her attention to the stage where Yehuda Glanz was now dancing about, changing instruments every five minutes.

"He's as hyperactive as my boys," she whispered. "How can he keep it up? I'm getting dizzy just watching him."

"Shhh!" repeated Malky emphaticallty.

Dizzy from Yehuda's antics, Bleemie turned in her seat to look at the balconies brimming over with people. On the highest tier stood little Mischa, jumping and swaying, his arm pumping over the rail, his grin stretching from ear to ear.

"Look up there, Malky," said Bleemie. Malky looked up to where Bleemie was pointing. "Aren't you jealous of my job, now?"

"Please, Bleemie, shhh! I want to hear the music."

The program flew by, finally reaching the part that Bleemie had looked forward to all evening. Heshy Rubin stood up to sing "These are the children."

"Listen to the words, Malky," Bleemie demanded.

"If you wouldn't be talking to me, it would be a lot easier," Malky hissed back in a stage whisper.

Bleemie pressed her lips together and settled back to listen, as Heshy sang of rabbis from different parts of the world. He was singing to the Russian children, inspiring them to be the next Jewish leaders. As each stanza of the song introduced another *Gadol,* one of the headlined singers would come on stage surrounded by a group of seven boys. The boys were wearing the bow ties, but Bleemie noticed some had managed to get out of the suspender requirement. By song's end, all of Bleemie's students were on the stage, joining the singing as Heshy passed the microphone from boy to boy.

Tearing her gaze from her students on the stage, Bleemie looked around the hall again. Most of the women in the audience, even those who she had suspected were here just for the social aspect of the evening, were crying as they watched the boys singing with the performers. Bleemie felt a lump in her throat, and a full feeling of thanks in her heart. She nudged her friend again. "Look, Malky, they do care," she said.

"Bleemie!" There was a distinct note of exasperation in Malky's voice. "What part of SH! don't you understand?"

The afterglow of the concert lasted for weeks. Her students constantly rehashed the whole event, describing the hall, the singers and the audience, invariably ending off with, "and they made us wear those silly bows!"

Three months later, Bleemie realized exactly how major the impact had been. Two boys, one her student, switched from the Yeshiva to public school. Bleemie called her former pupil every few weeks to remind him of his Jewish identity.

"Will you do something for me, Felix?" she once asked.

"What now, *Morah?*"

"Wash your hands the way I taught you to do every morning. Will you do that for me?"

"Fine." He didn't sound too enthusiastic about it.

A few days after that conversation with Felix, Bleemie and the rest of the staff arrived at school to find the place in total disarray. There were graffiti all over, books torn apart and thrown about — a terrifying scene of vandalism. Both staff and students were horrified and saddened when the police found that the ringleader was one of the boys who had left the Yeshiva.

"*Baruch Hashem*, Felix was not a part of this!" thought Bleemie. But why, why wasn't he? She knew that the culprit was his close friend.

She had to know, and that night she called him. "Felix, it's *Morah* Kleiner."

"What now, *Morah*?"

"Felix, I'm sure you heard about what happened to our school —"

"I swear I had nothing to do with it! I swear, *Morah*!"

"I know you didn't. And I'm very proud of you. But why didn't you, if you're so friendly with Yuri?"

"You know, *Morah*, remember the concert. At the concert I really liked being Jewish. When my friend's gang went to the school, they were screaming bad things about Jews. Like bad cursewords, you know. It didn't feel good to do that. Maybe I'm not religious, but it bothers me when people hate Jews — I go to public school, but I'm still a Jew. I even wash my hands like you told me to."

Felix fell silent for a moment. Bleemie held her breath, willing him to carry his thoughts to their logical conclusion. He continued thoughtfully, quietly, "*Morah*, maybe I'll become religious some other time. If I can play music like Yehuda Glanz and still be religious, maybe someday I will want to do that."

The concert did not just have an effect on her students. Bleemie, herself, had a lot to learn about life, and the event taught her a big lesson.

Her attitude towards American Jews had been self-righteous and indignant. She'd assumed that she was one of an elite few who really cared about Russian Jews. With immature harshness, she had dismissed the rest of the community as being too wrapped up in materialism to care. It was easy to feel that way far off in Russia, and certainly when she was overwhelmed with work here in America. Yet, slowly, she was learning more and more about the unbelievable caring a Jew has for another Jew.

Bleemie found herself saying, "*Mi k'amcha Yisrael*," with real intensity, as she kept meeting more and more people who genuinely wanted to be involved in helping Russian Jewry.

"You see," she explained to her ever-patient mother, "it wasn't that they didn't care. They just didn't know. Look how many people try to do all they can to help, once they're aware of the situation."

That Succos, Bleemie gained further insights into just how much people did care. On Simchas Torah, Bleemie took a group of "her boys," as well as Tanya and Miriam, *shul*-hopping. From *shtibel* to *shul* they went, in search of the ultimate Simchas Torah experience. In every place they visited, there were families who were so impressed with Bleemie's students that they volunteered to be host families to other Russian youngsters in the future. One *shul* was particularly attentive to "her boys," even giving one of them a chance to dance with a *Sefer Torah*.

"Morah, did you know that if you drop a *Sefer Torah* you have to fast? Man, I was so scared I was going to drop it," he said to her afterwards, adding that he had been invited back to the *shul* for a *Pirchei* program in the afternoon.

After Yom Tov, some of the people who had expressed interest in the boys actually called to follow up and make sure Bleemie had not forgotten their offers of help. Now some of her students had host families to show them the beauty of Shabbos. It was another turning point for her class, and Bleemie began to notice their progress.

"You have to show them, not just teach them," she explained to her mother, "because things like Shabbos have to be experienced to be appreciated."

Daniel was invited to the home of the Rav of his community and the Rebbetzin suggested that Bleemie come for a meal. As this Rebbetzin was a favorite of Bleemie's, she readily agreed. It would be fun to have a meal with Daniel.

Daniel was an earnest little boy, with brown blinking eyes behind very thick glasses. The Rav turned to him during the meal and asked him about his family.

"My father isn't around," Daniel announced conversationally.

"Where is he?" asked Bleemie. His mother had shown up to PTA with a man at her side, whom Bleemie had assumed was his father.

"Down under."

The Rav was puzzled. "He went to Australia?"

"Down under the ground. Buried." Everybody stopped eating and stared at the little boy. Daniel didn't seem to notice, continuing to eat his gefilte fish with zest.

"Oh —" said the Rebbetzin, pity in her voice, as she quickly put another piece of challah in front of Daniel. "How many years ago did he pass away?"

"Four years ago he died." Daniel looked up from his fish and picked up the challah. "Thanks. It's good challah."

"Were you close with him?" asked the Rav, trying to assess just how much sympathy would be appropriate at this point.

"He was not the kind of person I should know." Daniel waved his fork with a dismissive air. "You see, he died of a drug overdose." He took the last bit of gefilte fish into his mouth.

There were gulps around the table, then silence as all absorbed this bit of information. Bleemie wondered why any mother would burden a child with such knowledge, although she had to admit that the boy didn't seem particularly upset about the situation.

"That was good gefilte fish," he said to the Rebbetzin, nodding his head in emphasis.

The rest of the meal went more smoothly. "Good soup" and "Good chicken," as Daniel termed them, were accompanied by *Zemiros* and *Parshah* questions. Daniel outdid himself, joining in both.

"I'll tell you what, Daniel," said the Rav after benching. "If you come to my house every Shabbos, I will treat you to a day at FAO Schwartz."

"Cool." Daniel held up two fists, then offered the Rav a hand to shake, "Deal, Rabbi."

"Will your mother let you come?" worried the Rebbetzin.

Daniel frowned in thought for a minute. Then he nodded his head again. "For religious purposes she would definitely let," he said seriously.

The adults choked back their laughter. Daniel wandered off to the playroom. "Now, isn't he a great kid?" beamed Bleemie.

"Oh, my, yes," said the Rebbetzin. "I'm looking forward to getting to know him better."

Later that week, Bleemie had a long discussion with Daniel's mother, who saw his growth in religion as a means of keeping him from following in his father's ways. Daniel was given permission to spend every Shabbos and Yom Tov at the Rav's house, which became his second home. The couple enrolled him in a *frum* summer

A family for every child — that is what each of these Russian boys, studying in a Brooklyn yeshiva, needs.

camp and promised to get him into a good yeshiva after he became *Bar Mitzvah*.

"Now, if I can only find a family for every kid, it would be smooth sailing for me," Bleemie confided to her mother. But finding suitable host families for all her students was not easy.

Two students who were cousins were invited for a Shabbos by Bleemie's neighbor. After *Havdalah*, the neighbor called.

"Those boys are amazing. They really seem like regular *Yiddishe kinderlach*."

"Actually, they are regular *Yiddishe kinderlach*," answered Bleemie a bit stiffly.

"Yes, but you know what I mean. When I see Russians on the street, they seem so different, so pushy, always out to use people, to get things and they're not interested in becoming religious —"

Bleemie had matured a lot, but not to the point of being able to resist giving a lecture at the drop of a hat.

"Actually," she broke in, not wanting to hear the rest, "they just seem that way because we don't give them the benefit of the doubt. Don't forget that they were indoctrinated against religion all their lives. When you get to know them, you realize they are Jews, not Russians."

The crowning achievement of the Succos experience, thought Bleemie, was that six families offered to host girls from Kiev in their homes. That meant that more of her girls could soon come and learn and grow in America.

It was a juggling act, Bleemie often thought, but she was not willing to let go of even one child. Her stained-glass window glowed down at her, reminding her of the responsibility that she had undertaken in Kiev, and that she had to keep juggling to accomplish. Thankfully she was not alone in this task, because as more people became sensitized to the need, they took over part of the burden, shouldering some of the responsibility. As it had taken Bleemie a long time to learn, once people knew, they did care.

Chapter Twenty-Seven

∾ Matchmaker Matchmaker

A group of girls sat around the Kleiners' Shabbos table.
"C'mon, Bleemie, tell us funny dating stories," demanded Miriam, tossing a peanut to her former teacher.

"Let's see, h'm —" Bleemie struck a pose, hand on chin, then grinned.

"Did I tell you about the girl who didn't have navy shoes to match her new spring outfit? Just before the date she used a shoe dye from a spray can to change the color of her shoes. She thought they had dried, but obviously they hadn't, because when she tried to get out of the car her shoes stuck together, and she couldn't separate them. Imagine the picture! She couldn't get her shoes unstuck, so she couldn't get out of the car. When she finally managed to separate them, they certainly didn't match the outfit any more."

There was an outburst of laughter from Bleemie's listeners. "You made that one up, Bleemie."

"I did not," said Bleemie in mock indignation. "True story. I kid you not."

The girls laughed again, but Tanya was thoughtful. "I'm scared of what I'll have to go through to find the right *shidduch*."

"Stop worrying now. You're still a spring chicken."

"What's a spring chicken?"

"It means you're young enough to not have to worry now."

"Well, what about me?" asked Jana, one of Bleemie's night students who had become *frum* during her college years.

Bleemie was taken aback. "You're right! You've got to be thinking about it by now. But, don't worry, you've got so much going for you, who wouldn't want to marry you?"

"Yeah, but I'm Russian." Jana protested.

"So what? If I had your *middos* and looks, I wouldn't worry. You're a perfect candidate to be an *aishes chayil*."

Jana shook her head and looked down. "Who are you kidding? Nobody wants to date a Russian."

"Actually, I think that's untrue. I don't think most fellows would mind. I think the *shadchanim* are afraid to set up one nationality with another."

"You mean any boy would marry me?"

"No," said Bleemie. "It works like this: You have X amount of young men who would marry you. You choose among them. It's the same for me. Nobody with mega*yichus* or megabucks would think of me as a possible *shidduch*. I know such *shidduchim* are out for me. But I still have a whole bunch of boys to choose from. So, maybe you won't get a boy from a certain type of family; but I don't think your nationality will mean anything."

Bleemie looked at Jana again. "Come to think of it, you really do need to get married. I want to see you settled in a religious environment."

"You're telling me?!" Jana laughed. Then she grew serious again. "Nobody is suggesting dates for me, Bleemie."

When the girls had gone, Mrs. Kleiner looked at Bleemie in exasperation. "Bleemie, how smart is it to tell them these horror stories about dating? You're scaring them off."

"They're not half as scared as I am! Every time you tell me a *shadchan* called I start worrying what the next date will be like."

"Bleemie," her mother said in a disapproving tone.

"I mean the last chap said no because — quote, unquote — I was not *tzniusdik* enough about my *chesed* work!"

"And maybe you should consider whether or not that was a valid observation."

"Oh, so sorry, dear world, that I care about Russian Jews." Bleemie's tone oozed sarcasm.

"Bleemie, he did not say there was anything wrong about your being active —"

"So I should be happy he didn't tell me to retire from *chesed* work?"

"What he *did* say is that you don't have to wave it under people's noses all the time. Look, Bleemie, I know that being rejected hurts, but maybe there's something you can learn from it!"

"Mommy, I'm not arguing the matter any more. He's definitely not for me." Despite herself, Bleemie's voice revealed how painful the whole issue was.

Mrs. Kleiner decided to change the subject. "What do you think about Jana?"

Bleemie was in a bad mood already and out to paint the world black. "What will be with her? Everyone will set her up with losers because she is Russian."

Mrs. Kleiner gave up. A few days later she broached the subject again. This time Bleemie was in a better mood and more inclined to discuss the matter.

"Mommy, we've got to find someone for her. Nobody is setting her up. She has to get married. Her life at home is horrible because her parents are very negative about her *Yiddishkeit*. I want to see her settled already."

"Nobody has any ideas for her?"

"Nope. I tried to get Rebbetzin Friedman to set her up with the Steinbergs' cousin, the one who became *frum* through NCSY. It gets me so annoyed when someone asks why an American would marry a Russian. As if it makes a difference. I think it's a great match, but the Rebbetzin won't set them up because Jana is Russian."

"*Shidduchim* are not easy, Bleemie. Rebbetzin Friedman has made many matches and probably knows what would work and what wouldn't."

That last comment seemed almost like a dare to Bleemie. "I still think it would work, Mommy."

"So then go ahead and try to arrange it!" was the prompt reply.

Bleemie felt strange calling the Steinbergs, but that night she plucked up courage and made the call. They listened to her idea, and to her surprise did not say no. "We'll discuss it with Erik," they responded.

"That was a polite no, said Mrs. Kleiner, but a week later the Steinbergs called back to say that Erik was interested in meeting Jana.

"You know, I'm more nervous tonight than when *I* go out," confided Bleemie to Malky the night of Jana's first date.

The meeting went well. The next two dates went equally well. The fourth date was the best yet — Jana called while still with Erik to say that he had proposed and she had said yes.

"I don't believe it," said Bleemie to her mother. "Jana is the girl who once told me she would have to date for at least half a year before even considering marrying a guy."

"I guess when the right one comes along —" said Mrs. Kleiner with a smile. "May yours come along soon."

"Mommy, could you please not end every conversation with a comment about my future? I know that I'm single and need to get married. It's not pleasant to be constantly reminded about it."

Mrs. Kleiner sighed. "Bleemie, I think we should rehash the whole issue of your last date —"

"I've thought about it, Mommy. Well, maybe he was right. Maybe it sounds as if I boast too much about what I do. I just wish that people could realize that I'm not bragging, but that my work is me, this is a part of who I am."

"I know, *Mameleh*, but maybe lighter conversation would be nice on the first dates. Don't scare them off."

Bleemie grimaced. "Okay, weather and other inane topics, here I come." She stood, arms out wide in mock theatrical style.

"And now-introducing—the new, humble, quiet, meek, boring Bleemie."

Mrs. Kleiner smiled and shook her head. There was no quelling her daughter's exuberant personality. Somehow they would have to find a boy who would appreciate it, and not try to stifle it.

She looked at Bleemie in mock seriousness, saying, "And don't forget that this humble, quiet girl has a *shidduch* to be proud of — the meek *shadchan* at your call."

Bleemie smiled ruefully. "You know, Mommy, my pride and know-it-all attitude have always been my problems. I am trying to reduce them, but I don't want to cut out my work because of it. I'll just have to learn to be involved without announcing to the whole entire universe. The only problem is that I want other people to become active, too."

"Bleemie, at the expense of sounding like your many teachers, you know what Shlomo HaMelech said: 'To everything there is a time…' "

"So?"

"Dates are to get to know the person, not to rope him in to do work with Russians. Any other time you want to get someone involved is fine."

"You know how much help is needed — free dental work for my students, families to host my boys for Shabbos, lawyers to work out Jana's immigration mess and —"

Mrs. Kleiner laughed. "Bleemie, you're hopeless. We were discussing your dating, not getting volunteers."

"I know. But I thought we finished that subject. I'll behave on my dates from now on. Let the guys see the 'blah' me. Now I'm back to my favorite subject."

"Bleemie, Bleemie, Bleemie — I will be one very relieved mother when I see you safely under your *chuppah*."

"Uh, maybe you should call that *shadchan*, what's her name, Bleemie Kleiner, and find out if she has any eligible guys?"

"One match does not a *shadchan* make."

"Well then, I'm off to call Bella. Maybe I can think of someone for her too." Bleemie picked up a bottle and sang into it, "Matchmaker, matchmaker, that is me-me-me ME."

"Right, and don't forget that humility!" teased her mother.

Chapter Twenty-Eight

∞ Frum Kids Need Frum Schools

"**M**orah, Yitzchok's father killed a sheep."

Yitzchok was one of the few boys in the class who came from a *shomer Shabbos* family.

Bleemie didn't know if she really wanted to get into this subject, but realized it could be a learning tool. "Really?"

"Yes, he had the rabbi come and kill it," Yitzchok made a slashing gesture across his neck. All the boys were listening intently for a change.

"He *schechted* it?"

"And the rabbi blew up the lungs. Man, it was like a big balloon."

Her breakfast no longer sat so easily in her stomach. "Do you know why?"

"Nope."

"To see if it was kosher."

"But sheep are always kosher. Man, you should have seen its eyes."

"Yes, sheep are kosher. But you can't eat an animal that is sick inside. He was making sure it was healthy."

"And then we took out the brains."

Her food was definitely in her chest area by now. "Who *kashered* it?"

"The rabbi."

"The rabbi salted it?"

"No, my mother did that. We're going to eat it this Shabbos."

Bleemie laughed as she recalled that discussion. By now she understood Malky's assertion that teaching Bukharian children would be different. Not many teachers had students whose families *shechted* animals in their building's courtyard.

Two days later, Bleemie noticed Yitzchok standing with a group of boys who were dividing up their snacks. Something bothered her about the scene, but she couldn't figure out what it was. She went closer to the huddle of children and realized the snacks were not kosher! Bleemie swooped down on the unwary boys and confiscated the loot.

Yeshiva Academy had strict rules about bringing nonkosher food to school. The boys listened patiently as Bleemie lectured them about following rules. Par for the course. This kind of thing happened every day. But Yitzchok? Bleemie pulled him aside separately.

"How could you do such a thing, Yitzchok?" she scolded. "Your family just *shechted* an animal because you keep kosher and here in school you eat *treife*?"

"*Morah*, why are you yelling at me again and not the other boys? You yelled at me already when you yelled at them."

Bleemie realized it was unfair to the fourth grader to lecture him again. The environment was not right for him here at Yeshiva Academy. That afternoon, she discussed the problem with Rabbi Berlin.

"It's really a problem," he conceded, "but not many yeshivos will take in such a child."

"Even if his parents are religious?" Bleemie asked incredulously.

"Yes, even then. The only other option is trying to get transportation to get him to Far Rockaway. The yeshiva there will accept him."

"If Far Rockaway will take him, I'll find transportation."

To his parents' joy, Yitzchok was transferred to Far Rockaway Yeshiva. A month later, Bleemie bumped into him on the Avenue. She almost didn't recognize him. In dress, in manner, in speech, he looked every bit the *cheder* boy.

There was another boy in Bleemie's class who came from a *shomer Shabbos* home. Gavriel was extremely short and wiry. The schoolyard ringleaders teased him about his small stature, and he was largely ignored by the other boys.

Bleemie thought it strange, therefore, to walk into school one day and see Gavriel the center of everybody's attention. All the boys were slapping him on the back, standing around him, joking with him. What could have brought on this sudden popularity?

"*Morah*, did you hear Gavriel is going to be on TV?" asked one of her students, awe and respect in his voice.

This was certainly news to Bleemie, and within 15 minutes she had heard all the details from her excited students.

"He's going to be on the Bill Cosby show!"

"He won't have to come to school for a month!"

"He's a gymnast and will do stunts!"

"Only six boys in the entire United States were chosen — and he got the biggest part!

Rabbi Berlin and Bleemie discussed what their approach should be upon Gavriel's return from filming. The month was up, and the youth returned to school.

"So, Gavriel, what happened with your learning while you were away?" asked Rabbi Berlin.

"We had tutors on the set," said Gavriel.

"And he tutored you in *Mishnayos*?" asked Rabbi Berlin. "You know the *Parshah* this week?"

Gavriel blushed. "I did *daven* — even *Minchah*," he said quietly.

"Good boy." Rabbi Berlin pinched his cheek

Bleemie just shook her head in dismay. That night she asked her mother for advice.

"You can't tell him not to perform," explained her mother. "Of course you don't want your students to end up in Tinseltown, but if that's what they've chosen, you must make sure they do it properly. You know, maybe, you should have him meet Steven Hill."

"That's the actor who became totally *frum*?"

"Yes. Let Gavriel see that even if he becomes an actor, he still must keep the *mitzvos*."

"I heard the funniest story about Steven Hill," broke in Laya.

"Laya, must you sprinkle every conversation with your funny stories?" protested Bleemie.

"Hey, sis, admit it. You need me in your life for comic relief."

"Okay. So what's the story?"

"I heard that Mr. Hill was at a wedding in Montreal. Some man came up to him and said, 'Mr. Hill, I saw you on TV last week.' So he turns to the guy and looks him up and down. 'And why do you have a TV?' he thundered. 'It's *assur. Throw it out!*' "

Mrs. Kleiner smiled. "That sounds like him. It would be great for Gavriel to see he can't compromise his *Yiddishkeit* even if Bill Cosby chose him to perform."

"It's so hard for me. I can't imagine him continuing pursuing this as a career and, at the same time, holding on to what I'm trying to teach him."

"Of course you try to teach your students to aim for higher standards in their lives, but they're not all going to become *rabbanim*. At least let them have Shabbos and *kashrus*?"

"I hear what you're saying. I can't tell him not to perform. His parents want him to, he wants to — Do you think Rabbi Berlin will be able to hook Gavriel up with Mr. Hill?"

"Ask him. If he won't, I'm sure Tatty will find a way to do it."

"What would I do without you two," said Bleemie, giving her mother a quick hug. "Can we invite Gavriel's family for next Shabbos?"

"I don't see why not," said Mrs. Kleiner, returning the hug.

"Oh, but I do," protested Laya.

"You?" asked Bleemie.

"Yes, me," said Laya. "You're always out doing things for everyone, but I'm the one who ends up doing the extra cleaning."

"That's unfair. I pitch in, too."

"I don't notice you taking on more responsibility as you pile on more work on this house. You invite people, and I become their maid!"

"What's bothering you, Laya?"

"I just told you."

"Yeah, but that's not true. So what's really bothering you?"

Laya sulked silently for a moment, her back to Bleemie, then turned suddenly to confront her.

"You make time to help the whole world, but you never do anything for me! You promised to help me practice for my part in the school play. Did you? No. But I always have to be ready to help carry out your plans."

Bleemie took a moment to reflect before she answered. She vaguely remembered, a month or so ago, telling her sister that she would help her with her role in the school's major play. Laya, who was not as sure of herself as Bleemie, had only accepted the part after getting that assurance.

"Tell you what, Laya," said Bleemie, trying to assuage her conscience. "I'll do all the Shabbos preparations. Then, and she is even better than me, I'll have Ella coach you. She took serious drama lessons in Russia."

"But you forget," wailed Laya, "my performance is Sunday night!"

"Look, I'm sure that with Ella's help you'll do fine," soothed Bleemie.

"Easy for you to say. You're not going on stage to make a fool of yourself. This is my last year in high school, and I'd prefer not to make a grand exit by making a complete dunce of myself in a play."

"H'm – we can ask Gavriel for some tips that the television director gave him. Maybe some of it will be good for you."

"Right," muttered Laya darkly, "all I need is lessons from a 9-year-old kid."

⌒⌒

On Shabbos afternoon, Tanya knocked on the Kleiners' door. Bleemie had asked her to come over to help entertain Gavriel's mother during the long afternoon.

"Hi, Tanya," said Bleemie. "Come on in. You're just on time."

Tanya walked in, expecting to see a stiff, formal group of people making polite conversation. Instead she found Shimon Kleiner deep in a chess game with Gavriel. Mr. Kleiner and Gavriel's father were learning something together. Not one of the many Kleiner girls was in sight.

"Where is everybody?" asked Tanya.

"Wait 'til you see," Bleemie said. "Come."

The two girls entered the den. Mrs. Kleiner and her daughters were seated on the couch. Standing in front of them were Laya Kleiner and Gavriel's mother, Natasha. All were giggling helplessly.

"Sit near me, Tanya," invited Rechy, sliding over on the couch.

"What's going on?" asked Tanya.

Gavriel's mother used to be a famous actress in Russia. She's trying to show Laya how to do her part."

Tanya sat down, and Natasha continued going over Laya's role. The lady was indeed a star performer. Each bit of advice she gave Laya improved Laya's performance substantially.

"I can't wait to get on stage, now," said Laya as the lesson drew to a close. "Thanks!"

The Kleiner girls drifted out of the den in search of other Shabbos afternoon diversions. Tanya, Laya, Bleemie and Gavriel's mother remained in the room.

Bleemie introduced her friend. "This is Tanya. She was my student in Kiev."

Gavriel's mother smiled politely at Tanya. "Nice to meet you," she said.

Laya left to get more nosh, and Tanya and Gavriel's mother began making conversation. Soon they were discussing Shabbos at the Kleiners.

"You know," remarked Gavriel's mother, "we always kept Shabbos, even in Russia."

"Really?" Tanya did not know anyone else who had done that.

"*Dah.*" ("Yes."). But where we lived it was different than Kiev. In Southern Russia we still had a little more freedom. Most people kept something. We were even allowed to have a *synagoga*, so it was not so hard to keep Shabbos."

"Oh, you're from Southern Russia." Now it made sense to Tanya.

"But you know, our Shabbos, we really did not know how to keep. We just did not do work. But Shabbos here, today, it was with songs and learning and full of happiness. It was not just things you can't do. We never had that. Now, we learn how really Shabbos must be kept."

Tanya smiled at the woman. She knew exactly what beauty the woman had experienced today.

"Gavriel told us we have different Shabbos from the ones he sees at his school *Shabbaton*. Now, we will try to have the same Shabbos for him at home. It will take time — but we will learn. And then, you will be our Shabbos guest?"

Tanya smiled again, nodding her head in agreement.

Chapter Twenty-Nine

∞ A Time to Reap

"**P**hone call for you, Bleemie," called Laya Kleiner. "And don't be long. I am not scrubbing these pots by myself."

Bleemie grimaced. She put down the pot she was working on and rinsed her hands. "Hello?"

"*A gutten erev Pesach,*" said Rabbi Shteierman, director of Yad Yisroel.

Bleemie smiled. It was easy for the men to be cheerful about the days leading up to Pesach. After all, it was the women who scrubbed and worked their fingers to the bone.

"Now that you teach in America, you haven't forgotten the school in Kiev, have you?" asked Rabbi Shteierman.

"Not a chance. Why do you ask?" replied Bleemie, a sudden wild hope rising in her heart.

"Well, there is no meat and a severe shortage of matzah in Kiev for Pesach. We also need a teacher there. We were wondering — we know you can't go back to teach for long term, but maybe your parents would let you go for Pesach?"

Bleemie soon found herself on the plane with five tremendous boxes of food to be delivered to the Kiev community. Her parents had been supportive of the idea. Bleemie would be back in America right after Yom Tov. It was a perfect way for her to revisit her Kiev students, without neglecting her American ones.

Pesach was on Sunday night and her arrival time in Kiev was scheduled for Friday. It was a tight squeeze and Bleemie enlisted the aid of her travel-sized *Tehillim* to work it out.

The plane arrived on time. It took Bleemie two hours to *shlep,* tug, pull and push the oversized boxes to the front of the airport. There was no driver waiting for her. Bleemie wiped her flushed face and sat down to wait. The minutes ticked by quickly, yet still no driver appeared. Bleemie went to the nearest phone and dialed the *shul,* whose number appeared to be disconnected. Perhaps it was due to her frazzled nerves, maybe due to the hours of travel she had just completed, probably it was a combination, but try as she might, Bleemie could not remember the Bleichs' home phone number.

Alone in the airport with no driver in sight and no phone number to call, Bleemie (she, of brave, mature repute) sat down on one of her boxes and began to cry. It was not long before she had attracted the attention of every person in the airport. An airport official walked over and kindly escorted her upstairs to the Intourist office. Here the officials urged her to try calling again, which she did, to no avail.

"Hire one of our drivers to take you to the *synagoga*," suggested an official.

Bleemie knew such an arrangement would cost her. Intourist loved milking Americans for every penny they could.

"How much will it cost?" she asked.

"Thirty dollars."

Money was no object. It was the timing that was crucial.

"I would do it," explained Bleemie, "but I'm *religosa* (religious). I don't know what time sunset is here. I do know that under no circumstance can I travel in a car after sunset."

The Intourist officer smiled reassuringly. "Don't worry. You have plenty of time until then."

Was it the fact that he was a Ukrainian government official or just because he was a non-Jew that made Bleemie tend to doubt him?

"If the sun sets, I'm going to get out of the car and walk," threatened Bleemie.

"Okay, don't worry. I told you it won't set for another few hours." He obviously had a lot of experience dealing with frazzled, demanding American tourists. "Go, now," he urged.

Bleemie spent the entire ride into Kiev staring at the sun, willing it not to set. The man in the Intourist office had been right about the time. The sun was still high as the car arrived in front of the Kiev *shul*. She had made it. It was like coming home — the same tightening of heartstrings and the overwhelming urge to jump about hugging every familiar landmark.

After the excited greetings in the *shul* office, Bleemie was escorted to an apartment. She had an hour to make some semblance of order in the rooms before Shabbos.

But it was right after *Havdalah* that her real work began — *kashering* the kitchen and getting ready for *Bedikas Chametz*.

Her work was constantly interrupted by the girls who kept coming to visit her. Every time her doorbell chimed she had to stop her cleaning to hug another one of "her" girls. During a lull, there was a knock, and she opened the door without checking who was outside.

"Olga!" she gasped. She opened her arms wide, hugging the girl.

"I didn't know if you would like to see me," whispered Olga shamefacedly.

"Don't be ridiculous." Bleemie sniffled a couple of times, trying to stop the tears. "You're still my Olga."

It hurt Bleemie to see the girl in so much pain. It was obvious that she was torn between her two worlds and needed to explain her marriage.

"My husband really respects me for my Jewishness."

Bleemie winced.

"No. Really he does," Olga said quickly. Bleemie hadn't realized her emotions were so easily read on her face.

"Anyway, we're moving to Israel in half a year."

"Yeah, and once there, he'll divorce you," Bleemie thought bitterly.

She knew that many Ukrainian men married Jewish women just to get to Israel.

With all her reservations, and despite the pain, Bleemie still tried to make Olga feel like "old times" again, although they both knew it would never be the same. Olga could not live torn between two worlds.

When Olga had to leave, Bleemie invited her to come again. Olga smiled sadly and nodded — and both girls knew that there would not be another time, that as much as she had said she had not severed her ties, Olga was hostage to an alien culture. As much as she respected and loved *Yiddishkeit*, such a life was impossible with a non-Jewish husband.

Pesach was just as incredible as Bleemie had known it would be. Thousands of Jews in Kiev celebrated at community *sedarim* throughout the city. Bleemie, of course, took part in the *seder* for the girls' school, bursting with pride at the way the girls participated, sang and asked questions.

After Yom Tov, it was almost time to go home to America. Time to leave her girls — again. This second parting was even harder than the first.

As she hurried about, alternately packing and wiping her eyes, she heard a knock and flew to the door. There stood Tanya's mother and grandmother.

When Bleemie had taken Tanya out of Russia, she had had no idea of the magnitude of what she was doing. She had thought, naively, "I'll get her to America, let her live with the Steinbergs, grow up *frum* and happy ever after."

Witnessing Tanya's relatives' gratitude, mixed with their anguish at being so far from her, suddenly made Bleemie realize how people's lives interwine and how complicated it all was.

Tanya's mother, a former staunch Communist, married to a non-Jew, suddenly grasped Bleemie's hand, looked earnestly into her eyes and said, "I did not eat bread all Pesach for Tanya."

Bleemie felt a chill up her spine. What could this be if not the fulfillment of the ancient promise *"V'heishiv leiv avos al banim ..."*

"Tell Tanya we love her. Tell her we miss her but are happy for her."

Two generations of women smothered Bleemie in hugs and kisses — embraces they instructed her to pass on to their Tanya. They cried. Bleemie cried. They did not want to leave. Here was Bleemie, the only link to their Tanya.

When they had finally torn themselves away, Bleemie closed the door and leaned against it heavily.

"I feel so small."

The sound of her voice startled her. She had not meant to speak out loud.

It was time to write a thank-you note to the Steinbergs. Bleemie chewed on her pen thoughtfully, luxuriated in a few more hearty sniffles and began to write, the words and emotions flowing rapidly.

Dear Mrs. Steinberg,

> *I envy your Olam Haba. You should have seen her family's faces when I explained you did not get money for hosting Tanya — that you did it as a mitzvah. You not only have merit for what you do for Tanya — the way and reasons why you do it create a true Kiddush Hashem.*
>
> *I flew to Russia to "accomplish." It sounds exciting and most productive. But you, Mrs. Steinberg, there in America, in the "narrow" confines of your home managed to be mashpia, to truly accomplish in Kiev so many miles and languages away...*

Bleemie signed the letter and placed it in an envelope. She sat there at the table brooding. "I'm too young for this responsibility," she thought to herself. "Too young to bear other people's pain — too young to try to do *Klal* work."

She wondered if her heroes, Elimelech Tress and Rechel Sternbuch, people who had moved worlds, had felt so small and incapable. She suddenly realized they must have. And they did what had to be done anyway.

From generation to generation — the flame burns brightly.
Harav Avraham Pam, Shlita, with a student from She'arit Academy.

Bleemie squared her shoulders and sighed deeply. You will always feel small and incapable, she told herself. But Hashem knows, the work is so enormous, so painful, that in its presence you will always be small. Yet, if you dare to set out to accomplish, He will surely carry you forward on clouds of glory.